SMP interact 7T

I8

Practice for Bo

D0892743

Contents

CAMBRIDGE UNIVERSITY PRESS

PUBLISHED BY THE PRESS SYNDICATE OF THE UNIVERSITY OF CAMBRIDGE
The Pitt Building, Trumpington Street, Cambridge, United Kingdom

CAMBRIDGE UNIVERSITY PRESS
The Edinburgh Building, Cambridge CB2 2RU, UK
40 West 20th Street, New York, NY 10011-4211, USA
477 Williamstown Road, Port Melbourne, VIC 3207, Australia
Ruiz de Alarcón 13, 28014 Madrid, Spain
Dock House, The Waterfront, Cape Town 8001, South Africa

http://www.cambridge.org/

© The School Mathematics Project 2003
First published 2003

Printed in the United Kingdom at the University Press, Cambridge

Typeface Minion   *System* QuarkXPress®

A catalogue record for this book is available from the British Library

ISBN 0 521 53799 1 paperback

Typesetting and technical illustrations by The School Mathematics Project
Illustrations on pages 44, 96 and 103 by Chris Evans
Illustrations on page 56 ((e) and (g)) by David Parkins
Cover image Getty Images/Randy Allbritton
Cover design by Angela Ashton

③ Written addition and subtraction

Sections A and B

Do these without using a calculator.

1 (a) Show one way to make the highest total
  for this sum with the digits 1, 2, 3, 4 and 5.

  (b) Now do the same with the digits 0, 6, 7, 8 and 9.

2 Work these out.

  (a) 371 + 582   (b) 139 + 274   (c) 393 + 585

3 What is the highest total you can make when you add two 3-digit
  numbers made with the digits 3, 6, 8, 9, 4, 1?

4 Find the missing digit in each of these additions.

   (a)   567   (b)   6**?**3   (c)   851
        + **?**82   +985   + 7**?**3
      1049   1628   1644

5 This map shows distances in miles.

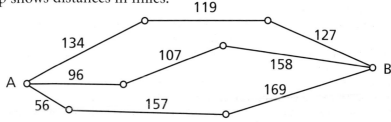

  (a) What is the length of the shortest way from A to B?

  (b) What is the difference in miles between the shortest and longest
   ways from A to B?

6 Work these out.

  (a) 678 – 47   (b) 362 – 139   (c) 444 – 177   (d) 560 – 415

  (e) 830 – 371   (f) 616 – 109   (g) 513 – 254   (h) 101 – 56

Section C

Do these without using a calculator.

1   Hedda gets £5.50 pocket money.
    She needs 88p for her bus fare.
    How much has she left to spend this week?

2   Work out the missing amounts in these bills.

(a)

Apples	60p
Carrots	30p
Brown loaf	70p
Total	?

(b)

Crackers	40p
Cruesli	£1.40
Trout	£1.10
Total	?

(c)

Haddock	£1.45
Peas	?
Potatoes	60p
Total	£2.40

(d)

Bacon	£1.70
Lettuce	?
Tomatoes	70p
Total	£2.59

3   Copy and complete this grid.

+	29p	£3.22	
34p			£1.50
£1.37			

4   (a) £1.36 + 78p   (b) 89p + £4.34   (c) 67p + £3.33
    (d) £0.94 + £3.21   (e) £6.42 + £1.87   (f) £5.55 + £2.88

5   (a) £3.37 − 22p   (b) £4.36 − 54p   (c) £6.91 − 74p
    (d) £9.87 − £3.43   (e) £3.42 − £1.56   (f) £2.12 − £1.67

6   (a) £3.28 + £4.92   (b) £5.37 − 83p   (c) 74p + £3.39
    (d) £5.79 − 38p   (e) £5.88 + £3.49   (f) £6.11 − £1.89

Reflection symmetry

Sections A and B

1   Jack has been drawing mirror images of some shapes.
    He put his mirror along the dotted line for each one.
    Which of these diagrams shows a shape and its mirror image?

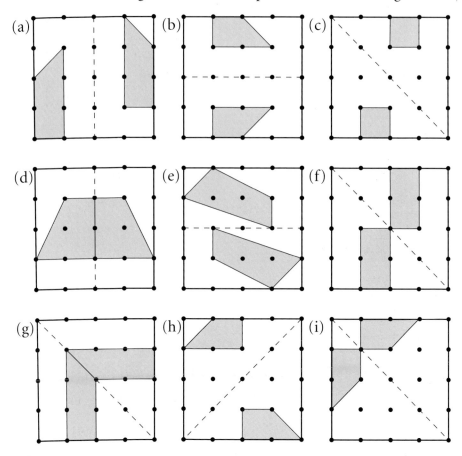

Section C

1   Here are some symbols from the railways of different countries.
    Which of them have reflection symmetry?

(a)   (b)   (c)

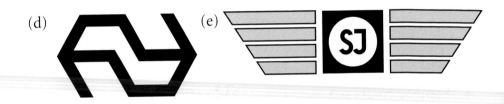

(d)   (e)

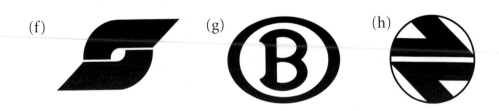

(f)   (g)   (h)

Section D

1   Some years have reflection symmetry when they are printed,
    for example

    -┼38┼-

    Which of these years have reflection symmetry?

1961	1881	2002	1331
1066	1301	1811	1812
1521	1380		

2   Find four more years that have reflection symmetry.

3   (a) Do any of the years in question 1
         have **two** lines of symmetry?

    (b) Find two more years that have two lines of symmetry.

4   Some sums are symmetrical: -┼8┼-+--┼0-

    Say whether each of these sums have one, two or no lines of
    symmetry.

    (a) 100 + 30   (b) 342 + 38
    (c) 18 + 81   (d) 83 + 38

5   Work out the answers to the sums in question 4.
    Are any of the answers to the sums symmetrical?

6   Make up some more symmetrical sums.
    Are any of the answers to your sums symmetrical?

Multiplication tables

Section A

Do these without using a calculator.

1 Copy and complete each of these.

(a) $3 \times 2 = ?$ (b) $2 \times ? = 10$ (c) $1 \times 3 = ?$ (d) $2 \times 2 = ?$

(e) $4 \times ? = 16$ (f) $5 \times ? = 20$ (g) $? \times 3 = 0$ (h) $10 \times ? = 30$

2 How many cakes?

(a)
| 5 cakes |
| 5 cakes |
| 5 cakes |

(b)
| 4 cakes |
| 4 cakes |
| 4 cakes |
| 4 cakes |
| 4 cakes |

(c)
| 3 cakes |
| 3 cakes |
| 3 cakes |
| 3 cakes |

(d)
| 2 cakes |
| 2 cakes |
| 2 cakes |
| 2 cakes |
| 2 cakes |
| 2 cakes |
| 2 cakes |

(e)
| 3 cakes |
| 3 cakes |
| 3 cakes |
| 10 cakes |
| 10 cakes |
| 10 cakes |
| 10 cakes |

(f)
| 4 cakes |
| 4 cakes |
| 4 cakes |
| 5 cakes |
| 5 cakes |
| 5 cakes |
| 5 cakes |
| 5 cakes |

(g)
| 3 cakes |
| 3 cakes |
| 4 cakes |
| 4 cakes |
| 4 cakes |
| 4 cakes |

3 Write down the answers to these.

(a) 2×4 (b) 3×5 (c) 5×2 (d) 4×3

(e) 5×5 (f) 3×3 (g) 4×4 (h) 0×3

4 Work out the score on each target.

(a)
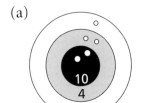

(b)
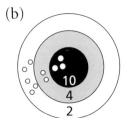

(c)
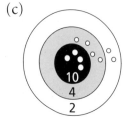

Sections B and C

Do these without using a calculator.

1 Each of these mixed-up multiplication
   tables uses the numbers 2, 3, 4 and 5.

Table A		
	2	3
4	8	12
5	10	15

Table B		
	2	4
3		
5		

Table C		
	2	5
3		
4		

(a) Copy and complete tables B and C.

(b) The total of the results for table A is

$$8 + 12 + 10 + 15 = 45.$$

Find the totals for tables B and C.

(c) Which table gives the biggest total?

2 Each of these mixed-up multiplication
   tables uses the numbers 3, 5, 6 and 8.

Table A		
	3	5
6	18	30
8		

Table B		
	3	6
8		
5		

Table C		
	3	8
6		
5		

(a) Copy and complete each table.

(b) Find the total for each table.

(c) Which table gives the biggest total?

3 (a) Make some mixed-up multiplication
        tables that use the numbers 4, 6, 7, and 9.

   (b) Which of your tables gives the biggest total?

Tables code

Each question below has two parts.
The two answers give you a letter in this grid.

For example, if you have written the answers
3 and 7, you get the letter H.

The letters will spell out five words.
The words can be arranged to
make a sentence.

	5	6	7	8	9
4	A	B	C	D	E
3	F	G	H	I	J
2	K	L	M	N	O
1	P	Q	R	S	T
0	U	V	W	X	Y

First word

1 (a) $8 \times ? = 0$ (b) $? \times 7 = 49$
   (Letter W)

2 (a) $7 \times ? = 28$ (b) $? \times 2 = 18$

3 (a) $6 \times ? = 12$ (b) $? \times 6 = 36$

4 (a) $2 \times ? = 4$ (b) $? \times 7 = 42$

Second word

5 (a) $? \times 6 = 6$ (b) $? \times 3 = 27$

6 (a) $8 \times ? = 32$ (b) $? \times 7 = 35$

7 (a) $? \times 3 = 12$ (b) $9 \times ? = 54$

8 (a) $7 \times ? = 14$ (b) $? \times 5 = 30$

9 (a) $4 \times ? = 16$ (b) $5 \times ? = 45$

10 (a) $? \times 1 = 1$ (b) $8 \times ? = 64$

Third word

11 (a) $9 \times ? = 9$ (b) $? \times 4 = 36$

12 (a) $? \times 5 = 15$ (b) $3 \times ? = 21$

13 (a) $6 \times ? = 24$ (b) $2 \times ? = 18$

Fourth word

14 (a) $? \times 3 = 6$ (b) $? \times 5 = 25$

15 (a) $? \times 8 = 16$ (b) $7 \times ? = 56$

16 (a) $? \times 7 = 14$ (b) $7 \times ? = 63$

17 (a) $4 \times ? = 0$ (b) $? \times 6 = 42$

Fifth word

18 (a) $? \times 7 = 0$ (b) $? \times 9 = 81$

19 (a) $8 \times ? = 16$ (b) $? \times 7 = 63$

20 (a) $8 \times ? = 0$ (b) $8 \times ? = 40$

7 Angle

Sections A, B and C

1 Write these angles in order of size, smallest first.

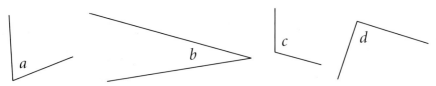

2 Is each angle of this shape acute, obtuse or a right angle?
Write *Angle p is ....* and so on.

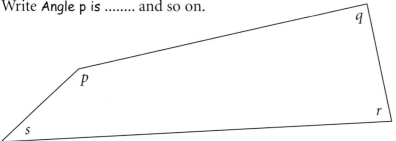

3 Copy this diagram.

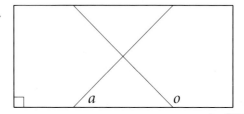

(a) Mark all the right angles in your diagram.
One right angle is marked already.

(b) Mark with an *a* every acute angle in the diagram.
One acute angle has been marked already.

(c) Mark with an *o* every obtuse angle in the diagram.
One obtuse angle has been marked already.

Section D

1 Copy this table.

Angle	Estimate	Real size
a		
b		
c		
d		
e		

Estimate the size of each angle below.
Write your estimates in the table.

Then measure each angle and write its size in the table.

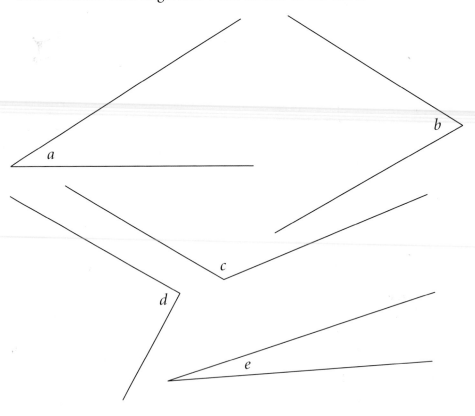

Sections E and F

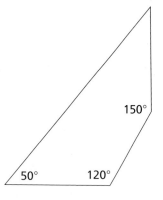

1   Draw a four-sided shape with three
    of its angles 50°, 120° and 150°.

    (a) Measure the fourth angle
        of the shape.

    (b) Add all four angles together.

2   Calculate the angles marked with letters.

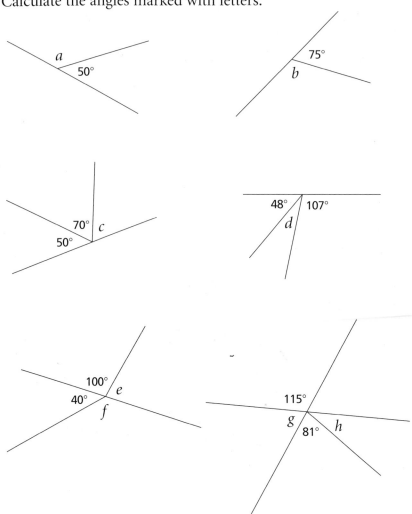

⑨ Growing patterns

Sections A, B and C

Squares are joined to make 'diagonal' chains.

1   This chain has 3 squares.
    Check that it has 10 corners.

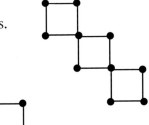

2   How many corners
    has this chain?

3   Draw a chain of 4 squares.
    How many corners has it got?

4   Copy and complete this table.

Number of squares	1	2	3	4
Number of corners			10	

5   (a) How many corners will a chain of 5 squares have?

    (b) Check your answer by drawing the chain.

6   How many corners will a chain of 10 squares have?

7   (a) Describe how the number of corners goes up as
        the number of squares goes up.

    (b) Explain why the number of corners goes up in this way.

8   A chain of 19 squares has 58 corners.
    How many corners will a chain of 20 squares have?

Section D

On a googlie plant where one flower grew, two flowers grow the following year.

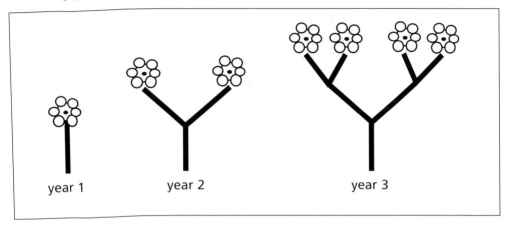

year 1   year 2   year 3

1   Draw the plant for year 4.
    How many flowers are there?

2   Copy and complete this table.

Year	1	2	3	4
Number of flowers	1	2		

3   How many flowers will there be in year 5?

4   Check your answer to question 3 by drawing.

5   Describe how the number of flowers goes up each year.

6   Explain why the number of flowers goes up in this way.

⑪ Fractions

Sections B, C and D

1 What fraction of each of these shapes is shaded?

(a) 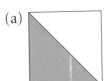 (b) 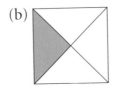 (c) 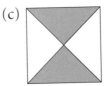 (d)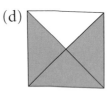

2 *This square is split into 4 parts.*
   3 parts are shaded.
   So $\frac{3}{4}$ of the square is shaded.

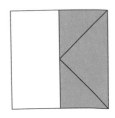

Is this right?
If not, what is wrong?

3 Say whether a half of each of these rectangles is shaded.

(a) 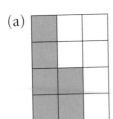 (b) 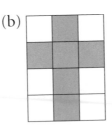 (c) 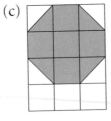 (d)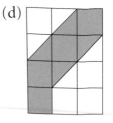

(e) 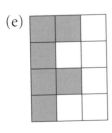 (f) 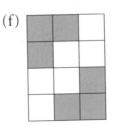 (g) 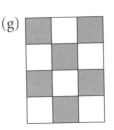 (h)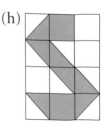

16

4 Say whether a quarter of each of these rectangles is shaded.

(a) 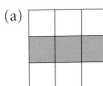 (b) 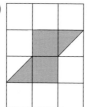 (c) 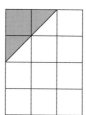 (d)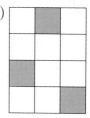

5 Say whether $\frac{1}{3}$ of each of these shapes is shaded.

(a)  (b) (c)

(d)  (e)  (f)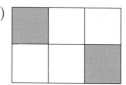

6 Say whether $\frac{2}{3}$ of each of these shapes is shaded.

(a) (b)  (c)

(d)  (e) 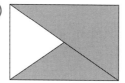 (f)

Section E

1 Write each shaded part as a fraction in at least two different ways.

(a) 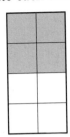 (b) 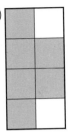 (c) 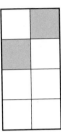 (d)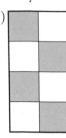

2 Make three copies of this diagram on square dotty paper.

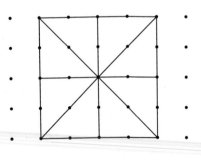

(a) On your first copy, shade $\frac{1}{2}$ of the square.

(b) On your second copy, shade $\frac{3}{4}$ of the square.

(c) On the third copy, shade $\frac{5}{8}$ of the square.

(d) Write the fractions $\frac{1}{2}$, $\frac{3}{4}$ and $\frac{5}{8}$ in order of size, smallest first.

3 In each of these pairs, which is the smaller fraction?

(a) $\frac{1}{4}$, $\frac{1}{8}$ (b) $\frac{3}{8}$, $\frac{1}{2}$ (c) $\frac{7}{8}$, $\frac{3}{4}$

4 Richard and David share a cake.
   Richard eats $\frac{3}{8}$ of the cake.
   David eats $\frac{1}{4}$ of the cake.

   Who eats more cake? Explain.

5 Write these fractions in order, smallest first.

   $\frac{7}{8}$, $\frac{1}{2}$, $\frac{3}{4}$, $\frac{3}{8}$, $\frac{5}{8}$

Mixed questions 1

Do not use a calculator for these questions.

1 The map shows four towns and the distances in kilometres between them.

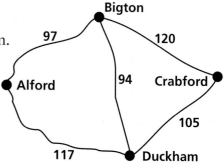

(a) What is the total distance between Alford and Crabford going through Bigton?

(b) How much further is it from Bigton to Crabford than from Alford to Bigton?

(c) Which is shorter – from Alford to Crabford through Bigton or from Alford to Crabford through Duckham?
How much shorter is the shorter route?

2 Words can have reflection symmetry.   ----DEED----   TOT

(a) Which of these words have reflection symmetry?

   MUM   **BOB**   **DAD**   **TUT**   **OXO**

(b) Which of the above words have two lines of symmetry?

(c) Find four more words that have reflection symmetry.

3 Copy and complete these mixed-up multiplication tables.

(a)

	5	4	3
2		8	
7			
4			

(b)

	6		4
5			
7			
8		24	

(c)

		4	8
3	21		
			40
9			

4 For each angle in this shape, say whether it is acute, obtuse, reflex or a right angle.

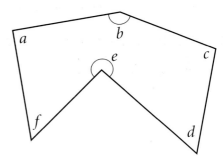

5 Calculate the angles marked with letters.

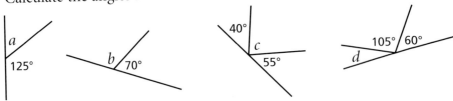

6 Suhel is making bracelets with silver rods.
Each section of the bracelet is a triangle.

This is a bracelet with 4 triangles.
He needs 9 rods to make this bracelet.

(a) Here are diagrams for the first three bracelets.

(i)   (ii)    (iii)

How many rods are used to make each bracelet?

(b) Draw a diagram for a bracelet that has 5 triangles.
How many rods are needed for this bracelet?

(c) Copy and complete this table.

Number of triangles	1	2	3	4	5
Number of rods needed				9	

(d) How many rods do you think will be
needed for a bracelet with 6 triangles?
Check by drawing a diagram.

(e) Describe how the number of rods needed goes up
as the number of triangles goes up.

(f) A bracelet with 19 triangles uses 39 rods.
How many rods will a bracelet with 20 triangles need?

7 In each of these pairs, which is the smaller fraction?

(a) $\frac{5}{8}$, $\frac{6}{8}$ (b) $\frac{3}{4}$, $\frac{3}{8}$ (c) $\frac{3}{8}$, $\frac{1}{4}$

⑫ Coordinates

Section A

1

Grid with letters A–Z plotted at points:
- A (0,4) B (1,4) C (2,4) D (3,4) E (4,4)
- F (0,3) G (1,3) H (2,3) I (3,3) J (4,3)
- K (0,2) L (1,2) M (2,2) N (3,2) O (4,2)
- P (0,1) Q (1,1) R (2,1) S (3,1) T (4,1)
- U (0,0) V (1,0) W (2,0) X (3,0) Y (4,0) Z (5,0)

Write down the letter at each point in the lists below.
Each set of points spells out a word.

(a) (3, 1) (2, 2) (3, 3) (1, 2) (4, 4)

(b) (2, 0) (3, 3) (4, 1) (2, 3)

(c) (4, 0) (4, 2) (0, 0) (2, 1)

(d) (0, 3) (2, 1) (3, 3) (4, 4) (3, 2) (3, 4) (3, 1)

2   Use the grid above to write down the coordinates for these words.

(a) SATURDAY   (b) NIGHT

3   Copy this grid on squared paper.
Mark these points and join them
up as you go.

(2, 5) (3, 3) (6, 3) (7, 5)

(7, 0) (6, 0) (6, 1) (4, 1)

(3, 0) (2, 0) (3, 1) (2, 2)

(1, 2) (0, 3) (2, 4) (2, 5)

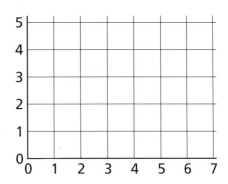

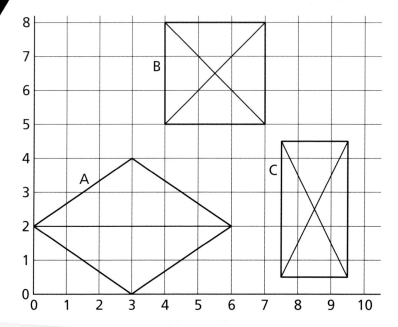

1 (a) Write down the coordinates of each of the four corners of shape A.

(b) What are the coordinates of the point at the centre of shape A?

2 (a) Write down the coordinates of each of the four corners of shape B.

(b) What are the coordinates of the point at the centre of shape B?

3 (a) Write down the coordinates of each of the four corners of shape C.

(b) What are the coordinates of the point at the centre of shape C?

4 For each point below say whether it is inside shape A, B or C or not inside any shape.

(a) (4, 3) (b) (8, 3.5) (c) (6.5, 7.5)

(d) (5.5, 4.5) (e) (2.5, 2.5) (f) (3.5, 0.5)

⑬ Area and perimeter

Section A

1 These shapes are drawn on centimetre squared paper.
   Find the perimeter of each one.

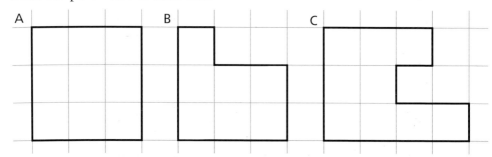

2 Find the perimeter of each of these shapes.

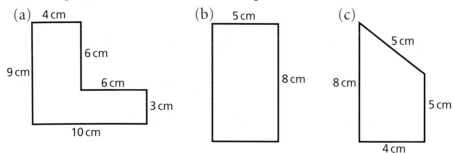

(a) 4 cm
     6 cm
   9 cm
     6 cm
     3 cm
     10 cm

(b) 5 cm
     8 cm

(c) 5 cm
   8 cm
     5 cm
     4 cm

3 This is a regular heptagon.
   It has seven sides.

   What is the perimeter of this shape?

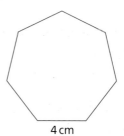

4 cm

4 A regular decagon has 10 equal sides.
   What is the perimeter of a regular decagon
   whose sides are 6 cm long?

Sections B and C

1   What are the areas of these shapes?

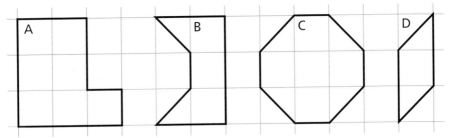

2   Work out the area of each of these rectangles.

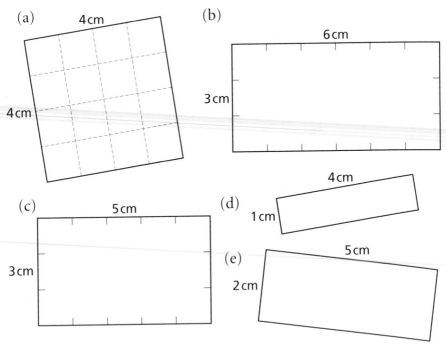

(a)   4 cm

4 cm

(b)   6 cm

3 cm

(c)   5 cm

3 cm

(d)   4 cm

1 cm

(e)   5 cm

2 cm

3   Find three rectangles with an area of 24 cm².
    Write down the length and width of each one.

Sections D and E

1 Write down the measurements of each of these labels.
   Work out the area of each one.

(a)

Chocolate coated
Bumble bees

"Really give you a buzz"

(b)

Reindeer Droppings

Chocolate covered novelties

(c)

PASTA POPS

The Long Lasting Treat

Genuine Italian Produce

(d)

ANGEL CRUNCH

The Heavenly treat that makes time fly !

(e)

CHILLY CHILLIS

Hot and cold sweets

(f)

Sardine Surprises

The new taste like nothing else

Sardines stuffed with marmalade and coated in chocolate

(g)

SAUSAGE DOGS

The longer frankfurter

Section F

1 For each of these shapes …
- Draw a sketch of the shape.
- Split the shape up.
- Work out the area of the shape.

(You may have to work out some missing lengths.)

(a)

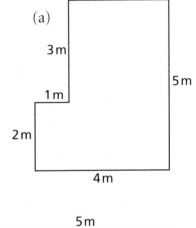

(b)

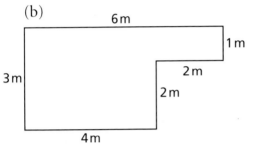

(c)

(d)

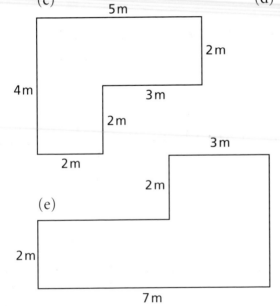

(e)

(f)

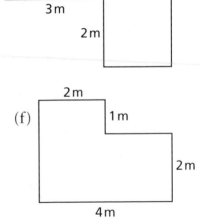

⓮ Rounding

Sections A and B

1 What does the digit 7 stand for in each of these numbers?

    (a) 672   (b) 1078   (c) 7004   (d) 3761

2 What number is

    (a) 10 more than 3457   (b) 10 less than 3457

    (c) 100 more than 3457   (d) 100 less than 3457

    (e) 1000 more than 3457   (f) 1000 less than 3457

3 What number is

    (a) 10 more than 7900   (b) 10 less than 7900

    (c) 100 more than 7900   (d) 100 less than 7900

    (e) 1000 more than 7900   (f) 1000 less than 7900

4 Work these out.

    (a) 4037 + 100   (b) 6295 + 10   (c) 5903 + 100

    (d) 2185 + 10   (e) 4099 + 1   (f) 6099 + 10

5 What number does each arrow point to?

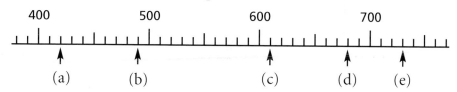

6 What number does each arrow point to?

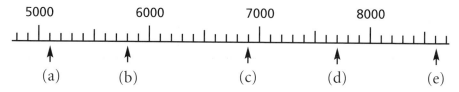

Sections C and D

1   What is the nearest ten to each of these numbers?

    (a) 62   (b) 79   (c) 45   (d) 129

    (e) 259   (f) 505   (g) 185   (h) 295

2   What is the nearest ten to each of these numbers?

    (a) 5713   (b) 6392   (c) 543   (d) 7071

    (e) 6450   (f) 3095   (g) 3398   (h) 2085

3   Round each of these numbers to the nearest hundred.

    (a) 3175   (b) 8933   (c) 5802   (d) 2963

    (e) 761   (f) 1777   (g) 5050   (h) 3950

4   (a) Round 3467 to the nearest ten.

    (b) Round 4193 to the nearest hundred.

    (c) Round 3964 to the nearest hundred.

    (d) Round 4204 to the nearest ten.

5   Sportsdesk has a competition.

> Guess how many people will attend the match at Grantham Town today.

The entries are

2284 2380 2231 2314 2394 2376 2351 2280

The club reports that the attendance is 2300 to the nearest hundred.

Which of the competition entries cannot be a winner?

6   Here are the populations of four places.

    North Caviston   2273   South Caviston   578

    East Caviston   3082   West Caviston   1966

Work out the total population of the four places and round it to the nearest hundred.

7   Work out the total population of these four places and round it to the nearest hundred.

Great Persham   3971   Persham St James   1840
Persham-on-Sea   4459   Little Persham   428

8   Round each of these numbers to the nearest thousand.
(a) 18 200   (b) 16 800   (c) 13 500   (d) 10 900

9   Round these to the nearest thousand.
(a) 12 780   (b) 23 560   (c) 22 880   (d) 21 090
(e) 34 562   (f) 23 891   (g) 43 921   (h) 29 231

10 Round each of the numbers in these headlines to the nearest thousand.

(a) | **12 965 flee war** |

(b) | **45 870 visit graves** |

(c) | **19 832 see UFO** |

(d) | **65 099 at Final** |

11 Round
(a) 2455 to the nearest 10   (b) 3165 to the nearest 100
(c) 7341 to the nearest 100   (d) 7341 to the nearest 1000

12 Choose the correct answer from the numbers in the loop for each of these.
(a) 755 rounded to the nearest ten
(b) 7500 rounded to the nearest thousand
(c) 750 rounded to the nearest hundred
(d) 7550 rounded to the nearest hundred

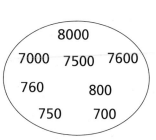

8000
7000   7500   7600
760   800
750   700

⑮ Mostly multiplication

Sections A and B

Do not use a calculator in this section.

1   Write down the results of these.
    (a) 32×10 (b) 32×100 (c) 256×10 (d) 256×100
    (e) 70×10 (f) 100×50 (g) 1000×20 (h) 25×1000

2   Copy and complete each of these.
    (a) $69 \times 10 = ?$ (b) $37 \times 100 = ?$ (c) $10 \times 45 = ?$
    (d) $10 \times ? = 700$ (e) $? \times 1000 = 65\,000$ (f) $? \times 100 = 5000$
    (g) $320 \times ? = 3200$ (h) $? \times 90 = 9000$ (i) $70 \times ? = 7000$

3   What different ways can you complete this
    using only numbers on the cards below?   □ × □ = □

| 30 | 42 | 10 | 3000 | 420 | 100 | 4200 | 1000 | 3 |

4   (a) Multiply four hundred and three by ten.
        Write the result in figures and then in words.

    (b) Multiply three hundred and nine by a hundred.
        Write the result in words.

5   Change these lengths in centimetres to millimetres.
    (a) 8 cm   (b) 55 cm   (c) 150 cm   (d) 500 cm   (e) 2500 cm

6   Change these lengths in metres to centimetres.
    (a) 7 m   (b) 35 m   (c) 125 m   (d) 800 m   (e) 3500 m

7   How much would you have left from a 5 kg bag of potatoes
    if you used these amounts?
    (a) 600 g   (b) 150 g   (c) 2500 g

Section C

Do not use a calculator in this section.

1 Write down the answers to these.

  (a) $220 \div 10$ (b) $4000 \div 100$ (c) $800 \div 100$ (d) $600 \div 10$

  (e) $50\,000 \div 10$ (f) $3000 \div 100$ (g) $3400 \div 10$ (h) $4900 \div 100$

2 £700 is shared equally between 10 people.
   How much money does each person get?

3 Write down the results of these divisions.

  (a) $320 \div 10$ (b) $8000 \div 100$ (c) $500 \div 100$ (d) $300 \div 10$

  (e) $5000 \div 10$ (f) $300 \div 100$ (g) $4500 \div 10$ (h) $75\,000 \div 100$

4 Find as many ways as you can of completing this
   division, using only the numbers in the box below. $\ldots \div 100 = \ldots$

400	30 000	650	25	300	65	4000
250	4	6500	3	2500	30	40	3000

5 Find as many ways as you can of completing $\ldots \div 10 = \ldots$
   using the numbers in the box above.

6 Write down the answers to these.

  (a) $120 \div 10$ (b) 120×100 (c) 100×20 (d) $100 \div 10$

  (e) 340×100 (f) 35×1000 (g) $2060 \div 10$ (h) 10×408

7 125 people live in Longdon.
   100 times as many live in Tewkesbury.
   How many people live in Tewkesbury?

8 Write down the answers to these.

  (a) $420 \div 10$ (b) 170×100 (c) 100×45

  (d) $1000 \div 10$ (e) 780×100 (f) 28×1000

  (g) $42\,000 \div 10$ (h) $350\,000 \div 1000$

9 Change these lengths in mm to centimetres.

(a) 350 mm   (b) 2500 mm   (c) 750 mm   (d) 5000 mm

10 Change these lengths in cm to metres.

(a) 4500 cm   (b) 7200 cm   (c) 700 cm   (d) 15 000 cm

Section D

Do not use a calculator in this section.

1 Work out each of these.

(a) 500×2	(b) 60×3	(c) 40×6	(d) 3×700
(e) 5×400	(f) 900×2	(g) 50×80	(h) 40×70
(i) 50×50	(j) 400×90	(k) 30×300	(l) 60×30

2 Find pairs of cards with the same answers.

30×80	400×6	30×60

10×20	20×90	80×2	5×40	4×40

3 Use just the numbers on these cards.

80	40	20	600

Find two numbers you can multiply together to make

(a) a number less than 1000

(b) a number between 1000 and 2000

(c) a number between 2000 and 4000

(d) a number between 10 000 and 20 000

(e) a number between 20 000 and 30 000

(f) a number greater than 30 000

Section E

Do not use a calculator in this section.

1 Find the areas of these rectangles by splitting each one into smaller rectangles.
Make rough sketches to show how you split each one.

(a)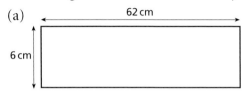

(b)

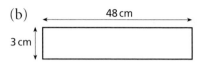

(c)

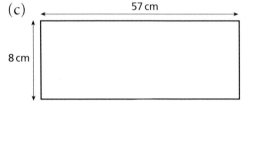

(d)

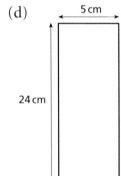

2 Copy and complete this table to work out 9 × 37.

×	30	7
9		

3 Use tables to work these out.

(a) 7 × 25   (b) 62 × 4   (c) 6 × 18

(d) 93 × 5   (e) 8 × 28

4 George spends £4 a week on lottery tickets.
How much does he spend in one year?

5 A car manufacturer completes 6 cars every hour.
The factory runs for 24 hours a day.
How many cars does it finish in a day?

6 Copy and complete this cross-number, without using a calculator.

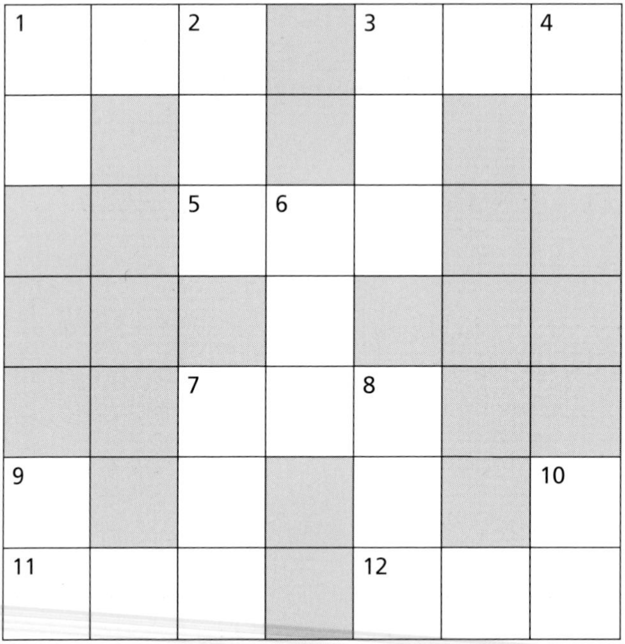

1		2		3		4
		5	6			
		7		8		
9						10
11				12		

Across

  1 62×8

  3 72×8

  5 5×36

  7 61×4

11 6×33

12 34×8

Down

  1 4×12

  2 93×7

  3 65×8

  4 16×4

  6 96×9

  7 36×8

  8 48×9

  9 3×27

10 24×3

Section F

1 (a) Copy and complete this table.

(b) Use the table to work out 15×36.

×	30	6
10		
5		

2 Work out 52×28 by filling in a table like this.

×	20	8
50		
2		

3 Make tables for these multiplications and use them to work out the answers.

(a) 24×28 (b) 14×32 (c) 37×16

(d) 26×54 (e) 56×49 (f) 74×12

4 Find the areas of these rectangles.

(a)

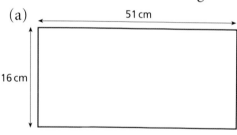

(b)

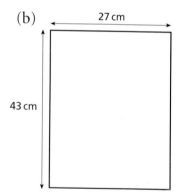

5 33 people take a trip to the theatre.
The tickets cost £17 each.
How much money is paid in total?

6 Sasha sews T-shirts.
She gets paid 24p for each T-shirt she sews.
How much does she earn for sewing 85 T-shirts?

7 Use tables to work these out.

(a) 24×314 (b) 18×423 (c) 35×414 (d) 244×36

Section B

1   All the scales balance.
    Find the weight of each creature.

   (a)

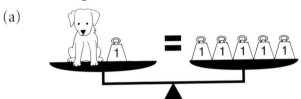

   (b)

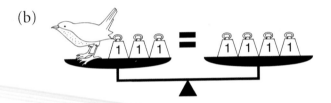

   (c)

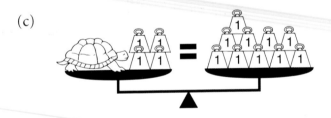

2   Each shoe weighs the same.
    What does each shoe weigh?

3 Each kettle weighs the same.
What does each kettle weigh?

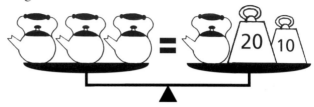

4 All the clocks weigh the same.
Find the weight of each clock.

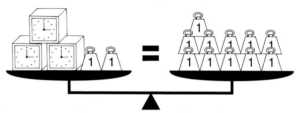

5 Both bottles weigh the same.
Find the weight of a bottle.

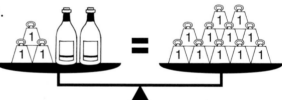

6 All the mugs weigh the same.
Find the weight of a mug.

7 All the jugs weigh the same.
Find the weight of a jug.

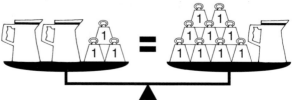

⑱ Gravestones

Rich Ancient Egyptians were mummified when they died.
These mummies can be examined and tested by scientists.
It is possible to work out the age at which
the mummified person died.

1   Here is a grouped frequency chart showing
    the age at death of 82 Egyptian males.

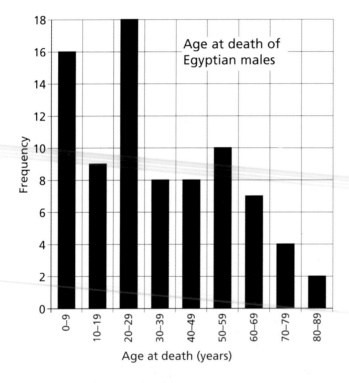

(a) How many males were between 30 and 39 years old
    when they died?

(b) How many males died before they were 10 years old?

(c) How many males lived 70 years or more?

2 Here are the ages at death of 59 female mummies.

23	6	19	21	4	10	17	22	20	30	17	35	18	27	3
25	30	21	1	25	28	40	21	14	40	26	36	50	6	9
11	25	4	20	35	21	18	35	3	52	19	23	20	21	33
21	17	36	40	54	55	4	70	25	60	22	29	16	96	

(a) Copy and complete this grouped frequency table for the females.

Age at death (years)	Tally	Frequency
0–9		
10–19		
20–29		
30–39		

(b) From your table draw a grouped frequency chart for the female mummies.

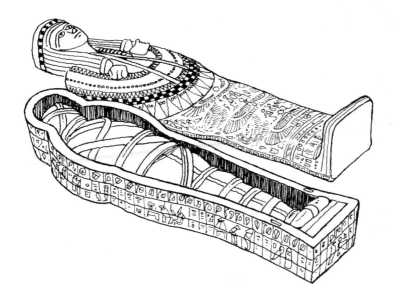

⑲ Brackets

Section A

1 Work these out without a calculator.

(a) $5 + (3 \times 2)$ (b) $(5 + 3) \times 2$ (c) $10 - (4 \div 2)$

(d) $(10 - 4) \div 2$ (e) $13 - (3 \times 3)$ (f) $(13 - 3) \times 3$

(g) $(20 \div 4) + 1$ (h) $20 \div (4 + 1)$ (i) $17 - (8 - 3)$

2 Copy these and use brackets to show which part is done first.

(a) $4 \times 3 + 2 = 20$ (b) $4 \times 3 + 2 = 14$ (c) $10 - 3 \times 2 = 4$

(d) $10 - 3 \times 2 = 14$ (e) $4 + 5 \times 2 = 18$ (f) $4 + 5 \times 2 = 14$

(g) $12 \div 3 + 1 = 5$ (h) $12 \div 3 + 1 = 3$ (i) $9 + 4 \div 2 = 11$

3 Match the words to the calculations.
One calculation can't be matched!

A Add 4 to the result of dividing 12 by 2.

B Divide 4 by 2 and add the result to 12.

C Add 4 and 12 and divide the result by 2.

D Divide 12 by the result of adding 4 and 2.

V $(4 + 12) \div 2$

W $(2 \div 4) + 12$

X $4 + (12 \div 2)$

Y $12 + (4 \div 2)$

Z $12 \div (4 + 2)$

4 Find the missing numbers.

(a) $(2 \times \square) + 1 = 7$ (b) $(3 + \square) \times 2 = 10$

(c) $\square + (4 \times 2) = 11$ (d) $9 - (\square + 2) = 4$

(e) $(\square \div 2) + 5 = 8$ (f) $12 \div (1 + \square) = 2$

(g) $2 \times (8 - \square) = 6$ (h) $10 - (\square - 3) = 6$

5 How many different numbers can you make using 2, 3, 4, +, ×
and one set of brackets? Use each digit or sign once only in each
calculation.

For example, $4 + (2 \times 3) = 10$

Section B

1 Here is an expression without brackets.

$$2 \times 6 - 3 + 1$$

Using brackets like this, its value is 7:

$$(2 \times (6 - 3)) + 1$$

Use brackets to make its value   (a) 8   (b) 4

2 Use brackets in the expression

$$12 - 5 - 2 - 1$$

to make its value   (a) 6   (b) 4

3 All the ways of putting two pairs of brackets into the expression $10 - 5 - 3 + 2$ are shown below.

Work out the value of each expression.

(a) $((10 - 5) - 3) + 2$ (b) $(10 - (5 - 3)) + 2$

(c) $(10 - 5) - (3 + 2)$ (d) $10 - ((5 - 3) + 2)$

(e) $10 - (5 - (3 + 2))$

4 Write down all the ways of putting two pairs of brackets into the expression $15 - 6 - 4 - 1$.
Work out the value of each one.

5 Write down all the ways of putting two pairs of brackets into the expression $5 + 2 \times 3 + 4$.
Work out the value of each one.

6 Use brackets in the expression $12 + 6 \div 3 - 1$ to make its value

(a) 9   (b) 13   (c) 5   (d) 15

Mixed questions 2

Do not use a calculator for these questions.

1 Copy this diagram on to squared paper.

   (a) Write down the coordinates of A, B and C.

   (b) D is the point (2, 0).
       Mark and label D on your grid.

   (c) Join A to D and C to D.

   (d) What name do we give to the shape
       that is made by A, B, C and D?

   (e) Draw the diagonals of the shape.

   (f) Write down the coordinates of the point
       where the diagonals cross.

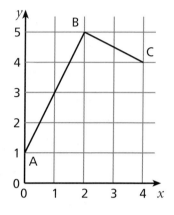

2 Find the perimeter and area of each of these shapes.

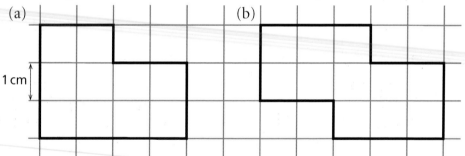

(a)

(b)

1 cm

3 Work out the perimeter and area of each of these.

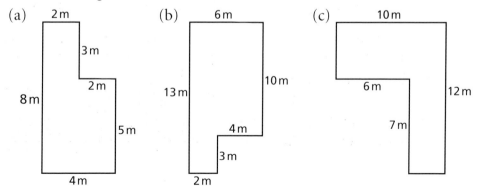

(a) 2 m, 3 m, 2 m, 8 m, 5 m, 4 m

(b) 6 m, 13 m, 10 m, 4 m, 2 m, 3 m

(c) 10 m, 6 m, 12 m, 7 m

4 What does the figure 3 stand for in each of these numbers?

    (a) 1030   (b) 1300   (c) 3100   (d) 9131

5 Round each of these numbers.

    (a) 6521 to the nearest hundred   (b) 14 534 to the nearest thousand

    (c) 5345 to the nearest ten   (d) 2432 to the nearest hundred

6 Write down the results of these.

    (a) 36×10 (b) 10×43 (c) 100×21 (d) 100×650

    (e) 10×600 (f) 1000×54 (g) 20×40 (h) 400×20

    (i) $520 \div 10$ (j) $5000 \div 100$ (k) $6700 \div 10$ (l) $80\,000 \div 1000$

7 Change each of these.

    (a) 15 m to cm   (b) 60 m to cm   (c) 200 cm to m

    (d) 1500 cm to m   (e) 5 kg to g   (f) 8000 g to kg

8 Work out these.

    (a) 423×4 (b) 43×34 (c) 67×52 (d) 23×72

9 Find the weight of a tin in each of these pictures.

(a) 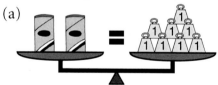   (b)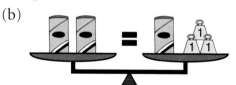

10 Work out each of these.

    (a) $8 + (2 \times 5)$ (b) $20 - (3 \times 4)$ (c) $3 \times (5 - 1)$ (d) $(6 + 1) \times 3$

11 The chart shows the ages of some children in hospital.

    (a) How many children were aged between 6 and 8?

    (b) What was the age group with most children in hospital?

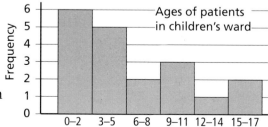

20 Lines at right angles

Sections A and B

1 How many degrees are there in a right angle?

2 The hour hand on this clock is pointing to 2.

(a) What number will it point to if it turns through a right angle clockwise?

(b) What number will the hour hand point to if it turns from 2 through a right angle anticlockwise?

3 To answer this question, you may find it useful to make a sketch of the eight points of the compass.

(a) Imagine you are facing north. You turn through a right angle clockwise. Which compass direction are you facing in now?

(b) You are facing north again. You turn through a right angle anticlockwise. Which direction are you facing in now?

(c) Imagine you are facing south-east. You turn through a right angle clockwise. What direction are you now facing?

(d) Imagine you are facing west. You turn though half a right angle clockwise. What direction are you facing in?

(e) You are facing north-west. You turn through two right angles clockwise. What direction are you facing in now?

44

4   Here are some sketches of shapes.
    Draw them accurately on plain paper.
    You can use the corner of a piece of paper to draw the right angles.

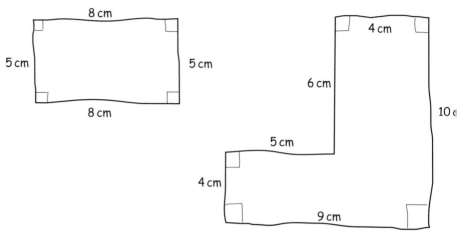

5   Here are 11 lines. There are 5 pairs which are perpendicular.
    Use the corner of a piece of paper to decide
    which of the lines are perpendicular.

    Which line is the odd one out?

a

b

c

d

e

f

g

h

i

j

k

21 Division

Section B

Break the code

Start at the square marked A.

Do each calculation.
The answer tells you which
direction to go to a new square:

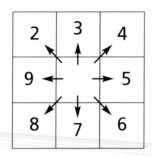

M	P	I	D	G
U	R	T	N	B
E	S	**A**	T	E
T	Y	T	G	R
R	E	O	U	L

As you go from square to square you will spell
out a message. (Remember to start at **A.**)

1   $10 \div 5$ (The answer is 2 so move this way ↖ to letter R.)

2   $16 \div 2$ (The answer is 8 so move this way from R ↙ to letter E.)

3 $24 \div 4$	**4** $42 \div 7$	**5** $25 \div 5$	**6** $24 \div 8$
7 $36 \div 9$	**8** $18 \div 2$	**9** $14 \div 7$	**10** $18 \div 6$
11 $54 \div 9$	**12** $28 \div 7$	**13** $63 \div 9$	**14** $28 \div 4$
15 $63 \div 7$	**16** $72 \div 9$	**17** $40 \div 5$	**18** $81 \div 9$

Section C

1   Oranges are packed in bags of 3.
    How many bags will these oranges fill?

2   Eggs are packed in boxes of 6.
    How many boxes will these eggs fill?

3   Max has 18 eggs. He puts them in boxes of 6.
    How many boxes does he fill?

4   Ajit has 25 buttons. He sews them on to cards.
    Each card needs 5 buttons.
    How many cards does he fill?

5   20 people go on a picnic. They go in cars.
    Each car holds 4 people.
    How many cars do they need?

6   30 girls play five-a-side football. Each team has 5 girls in it.
    How many teams can they make up?

7   Tina has 28 postcards. She puts them into envelopes.
    Each envelope holds 4 cards.
    How many envelopes does she need?

8   Rahima is packing lemons into baskets. She has 36 lemons.
    She puts 4 lemons into each basket.
    How many baskets can she fill?

Section D

1 25 sweets are shared equally between 5 people.
   How many sweets does each person get?

2 Chocolate bars are sold in packs of 4.
   How many packs can be made from 28 chocolate bars?

3 4 people have a meal. They share the cost equally.
   The meal costs £44. How much does each person pay?

4 6 people have a meal. They share the cost equally.
   The meal costs £54. How much does each person pay?

5 Flo has 40 buttons. She sews them on to cards.
   Each card needs 8 buttons.
   How many cards does she fill?

6 45 girls play five-a-side football. Each team has 5 girls in it.
   How many teams can they make up?

In these questions you must decide whether to add, subtract, multiply or divide.

7 2 friends are collecting for charity.
   Sam collects 35p. Jo collects 23p.
   How much have they collected altogether?

8 Luis wants to buy 42 crackers. There are 6 crackers in a box.
   How many boxes must he buy?

9 Pat has 36 cats. Mary has 61 cats.
   How many more cats does Mary have than Pat?

10 One large tin of cat food feeds 6 cats.
    How many tins will Pat need to feed her 36 cats?

11 Maria has 9 goldfish.
    Candy has twice as many goldfish as Maria.
    How many goldfish do Maria and Candy have altogether?

Section E

1 Do these divisions have remainders? Write 'Yes' or 'No' for each one.
   (a) $16 \div 3$ (b) $21 \div 4$ (c) $32 \div 8$ (d) $17 \div 5$

2 Work out each of these. Write your answers like this:
   '2(a) $22 \div 5 = 4$ rem 2'
   (a) $22 \div 5$ (b) $17 \div 2$ (c) $9 \div 2$ (d) $20 \div 3$

3 Work these out.
   (a) $30 \div 6$ (b) $27 \div 8$ (c) $25 \div 6$ (d) $40 \div 7$

4 Work these out.
   (a) $39 \div 8$ (b) $23 \div 7$ (c) $65 \div 10$
   (d) $35 \div 8$ (e) $21 \div 9$ (f) $43 \div 6$

5 Stella has 34 bangles to put into bags. Each bag holds 5 bangles.
   (a) How many bags can she fill?   (b) How many bangles are left over?

6 Jo is fitting new tyres to model racing cars.
   Each car needs 4 tyres. He has 23 new tyres.
   (a) How many cars can he fit with new tyres?
   (b) How many tyres will be left over?

7 Kim has 3 horses and 20 lumps of sugar.
   She shares the sugar lumps equally between the horses.
   (a) How many lumps does each horse get?
   (b) How many lumps are left over?

8 6 children share 50 Smarties. How many can they have each,
   and how many are left over?

9 8 grannies share 35 tea-cakes. How many can they have each?
   How many are left over?

10 3 gardeners share 20 garden gnomes. How many do they get each?
    How many gnomes are left over?

Section F

1 Matt is putting tins of fruit into old peoples' Christmas boxes.
He has 325 tins of fruit and he puts 5 tins into each box.
How many boxes can he put fruit into?

2 Ian makes furniture. Each table he makes needs 4 legs.
He has 110 table legs. How many tables can he make?
Will he have any legs left over? If so, how many?

3 Ian also makes stools. Each stool needs 3 legs.
He has 100 legs for stools. How many stools can he make?
Will he have any stool legs left over? If so, how many?

4 Mike is putting paintbrushes into packets. Each packet takes 6 brushes.
He has 225 brushes. How many packets can he fill?
Will he have any brushes left over? If so, how many?

5 Jan puts 74 iced buns into cardboard boxes. Each box holds 3 buns.
How many cardboard boxes can she fill?
Will she have any buns left over? If so, how many?

6 Rajan has 87 toy cars. He wants to give them to 3 charity shops.
How many cars can he give to each shop?
Will there be any toy cars left over? If so, how many?

7 Share 250 stamps equally between 6 children. Are any left over?

8 Can you share 342 bones equally between 3 dogs, with none left over?

9 Diane has 100 hats. Work out how many hats each person gets, and
how many hats are left over, if she shares them between

(a) 2 people   (b) 3 people   (c) 5 people   (d) 6 people

10 Work out each of these. Say what the remainder is, if there is one.

(a) $130 \div 3$ (b) $243 \div 6$ (c) $305 \div 2$ (d) $200 \div 7$

(e) $243 \div 8$ (f) $150 \div 4$ (g) $350 \div 4$ (h) $500 \div 3$

Section G

1 For my birthday party I want to buy 33 paper hats.
The hats come in packets of 5.
How many packets must I buy?

2 I also need to buy 33 plastic spoons.
The spoons come in packets of 10.
How many packets of spoons will I need?

3 I was given 28 creme eggs for my birthday.
I put the eggs into boxes, with 6 eggs in each box.
How many boxes did I fill completely?

4 I need to cook 130 sausage rolls. My oven only holds 8 rolls.
How many times will I need to use the oven to cook all the rolls?

5 6 boys share 570 stamps equally. 8 girls share 690 stamps.
Who gets more stamps, each boy or each girl?

6 4 friends pick apples. They pick 37, 43, 29 and 44 apples.
They decide to put them together and share them out equally.

   (a) How many apples do they each get?

   (b) How many more do they need to pick to avoid
       having any left over?

7 Sadia needs 180 litres of water to fill her pond.
She takes water to the pond in a bucket which holds 8 litres.
How many times will she have to use the bucket?

*8 John is making concrete. To fill his mixer he needs
      6 buckets of gravel,
      4 buckets of sand and
      2 buckets of cement.
   He has got 117 buckets of gravel, 83 buckets of sand and
   49 buckets of cement.
   How many times can he fill his mixer?

Parallel lines

Sections A and B

1 (a) Which of the lines *p*, *q*, *r*, *s*, *t* and *u* is parallel to line *v*?

(b) Which line is parallel to *q*?

(c) Find a set of three parallel lines in the diagram.

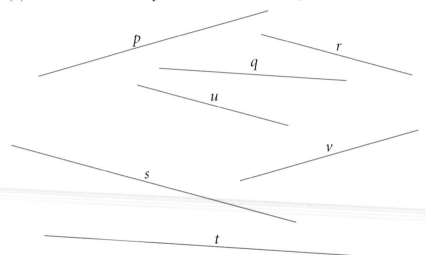

2 (a) In this diagram, *a* is parallel to *f*.
Which other line is parallel to *a*?

(b) Write down another set
of three parallel lines.

(c) Which line is not parallel to
any of the other lines?

(d) Which line is parallel to *e*?

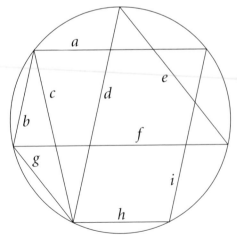

3 This shape has three pairs
of parallel sides.
Which are they?

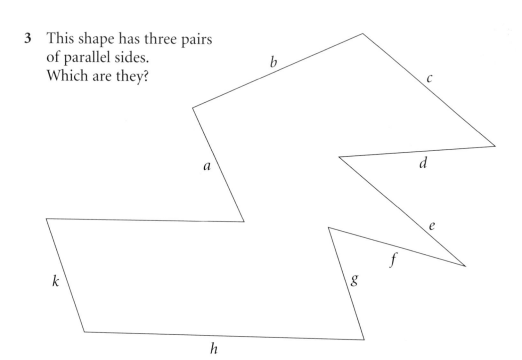

4 Use plain paper for this question.

Draw a triangle with sides about 15 cm long – you need not be exact.
Now draw a pattern like this one.
Each pair of parallel lines
must be exactly 1 cm apart.

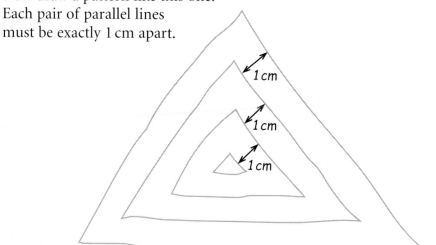

Section C

1 Are the two thick lines parallel?

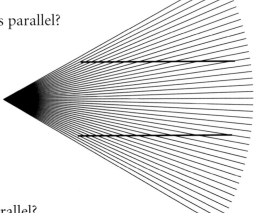

2 Are these two lines parallel?

3 One of these lines is parallel to *a*. Which is it?

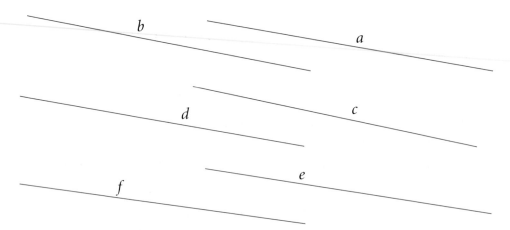

㉓ Time

Section C

1   Look at the times on these cards.
    Write down the letters of the cards which show the same time.
    Write your answers like this: 'A and ...'

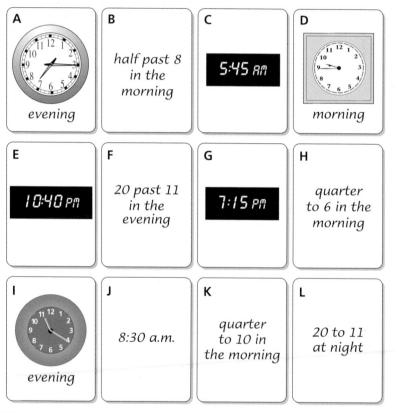

A evening	**B** half past 8 in the morning	**C** 5:45 AM	**D** morning
E 10:40 PM	**F** 20 past 11 in the evening	**G** 7:15 PM	**H** quarter to 6 in the morning
I evening	**J** 8:30 a.m.	**K** quarter to 10 in the morning	**L** 20 to 11 at night

2   We can write 'a quarter to 7 in the morning' as 6:45 a.m.
    Write these times using a.m. or p.m.

(a) Half past 6 in the morning   (b) A quarter past 10 at night

(c) A quarter to 9 at night   (d) 20 to 8 in the morning

(e) 25 minutes to 10 at night   (f) 10 to 10 in the morning

(g) 5 to 3 in the afternoon   (h) 5 past 5 in the morning

Sections D and E

1   Allie is at Bush Street School.
    On Mondays, school starts at 8:50 a.m.

   (a) Allie is in her tutor group
      from 8:50 a.m. until 9:05 a.m.
      How long is that?

   (b) Assembly starts at 9:05 a.m. and
      lasts until 9:30 a.m.
      How many minutes does assembly last?

   (c) The first lesson is maths.
      It starts at 9:30 a.m. and goes on until 10:25 a.m.
      How long is the maths lesson?

   (d) Break starts at 10:25 a.m. and lasts until 10:45 a.m.
      How long is break?

   (e) Science starts at 10:45 a.m.
      It ends at 12:10 p.m.
      How long is science?

   (f) Lunch begins at 12:10 p.m. and lasts until 1:40 p.m.
      How long does lunch last?

   (g) PE starts at 1:40 p.m. ...   ... and ends at 3:10 p.m.

      How long does PE last?

   (h) How long is it from the start of school until the end of PE?

   (i) Allie goes to a friend's house. She gets there at a quarter to four.
      She leaves at 6:20 p.m.
      How long is she at her friend's house?

2 Jan goes to see *Robocat II* at the cinema.
She gets to the cinema at 10 past 7.

> **Robocat II**
> starts
> 7:30 p.m.

(a) The film starts at 7:30 p.m.
How long does she wait for the film to start?

(b) The film is in two parts.
The first part ends at a quarter to 9.
How long does the first part last?

(c) The interval lasts from a quarter to 9 until 9:05 p.m.
How long is the interval?

(d) The film ends at 5 minutes to 10.
How long is the second part?

(e) For how long was Jan at the cinema altogether?

3 How long is it from

(a) 10:45 a.m. to 11:30 a.m.   (b) 9:10 a.m. to 10:30 a.m.

(c) 9:40 a.m. to 11:00 a.m.   (d) 3:15 p.m. to 5:00 p.m.

(e) 3:45 p.m. to 6:30 p.m.   (f) noon to 1:20 p.m.

4 (a) Sarah gets to the station at 6:45 a.m.
How long does she have to wait for
the next train?

(b) Gary gets to the station at a quarter to 9.
How long does he have to wait for a train?

(c) Jade leaves home at a quarter past 10.
How long is it to the next train?

> **Trains leave at**
> 7:30 a.m.
> 8:15 a.m.
> 8:55 a.m.
> 10:00 a.m.
> 11:45 a.m.
> 1:30 p.m.

5 This is a train timetable from Cargate.

(a) How long does the train take from Cargate
to Figgleswick?

(b) How long does it take from Oggle to Yain?

(c) I get to Gamsway at quarter to 11.
How long do I have to wait for the train?

(d) I get to Wyre Links at 10 past 11.
How long will it be until I get to Rumkittle?

Cargate	10:15
Mapborough	10:25
Figgleswick	10:45
Gamsway	11:05
Oggle	11:10
Wyre Links	11:25
Yain	11:35
Poddlebod	11:45
Rumkittle	11:55

Section F

1 Copy and complete this table.

12-hour clock	24-hour clock
8 p.m.	
	09:45
3:40 p.m.	
	17:25
9:55 a.m.	
	23:15

2 This is a timetable for coaches from a London coach station.

Destination	Departs	Arrives
Bath	11:30	14:45
Cambridge	13:20	15:10
Cirencester	12:20	14:25
Dover	14:00	16:45
Edinburgh	09:15	17:45
Liverpool	11:15	16:15
York	17:20	21:50

(a) (i) At what time does the coach for Dover depart?

(ii) At what time does it arrive?

(iii) How long does the coach take from London to Dover?

(b) How long does each of these coach journeys take from London?

(i) Liverpool　　(ii) Edinburgh　　(iii) Cambridge

(c) Sally is getting the coach to Bath.
Her mum says she will pick her up in Bath at 3 p.m.
How long will Sally have to wait for her mum?

(d) The coach company plans to run an overnight service to Glasgow.
The journey to Glasgow takes 7 hours and 45 minutes.

If the coach leaves at 11:30 p.m.,
what time would it arrive in Glasgow?

(e) Ewan is catching the coach from London to Edinburgh.
He arrives at the coach station at 8:40 a.m.
How long is it until the Edinburgh coach leaves?

㉔ Work to rule

Friezes are made with decorative tiles. This tile is used.

Here are some friezes.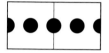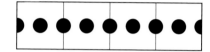

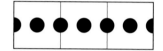 

1   Look at the frieze with 2 tiles.
How many whole circles are there? (Don't include bits of circles.)

2   Look at the frieze with 4 tiles. How many whole circles are there?

3   Sketch a frieze with 5 tiles. How many whole circles are there?

4   Copy and complete this table.

Number of tiles	1	2	3	4	5	6
Number of circles			5			

5   (a) Describe how the number of circles goes up
as the number of tiles goes up.

    (b) Explain why the number of circles goes up in this way.

6   How many circles would there be in a frieze with
(a) 8 tiles   (b) 10 tiles

7   How many circles would there be in a frieze with 100 tiles?

8   Explain how you can find the number of circles
if you know the number of tiles.

9   Work out how many circles there would be in a frieze with 150 tiles.

This tile is used to make some friezes.

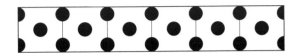

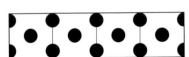

10 How many whole circles are there in the frieze with 6 tiles?

11 Sketch a frieze with 2 tiles. How many whole circles are there?

12 Sketch a frieze with 5 tiles. How many whole circles are there?

13 How many whole circles are there in a frieze with 7 tiles?

14 Copy and complete this table.

Number of tiles	1	2	3	4	5	6	7
Number of circles			7				

15 (a) Without drawing, how many whole circles would
          there be in a frieze with 10 tiles?

    (b) Check your results by sketching a frieze with 10 tiles.

16 How many circles would there be in a frieze with 20 tiles?

17 How many circles would there be in a frieze with 50 tiles?

18 Explain how you can find the number of whole
circles in a frieze if you know the number of tiles.

19 Work out how many whole circles would be in a frieze with
    (a) 25 tiles   (b) 42 tiles

25 One decimal place

Section A

1 These are some full-size drawings of the world's smallest mammals.

(a) Estimate the length of each mammal in cm.

(b) Measure the length of each mammal in cm.

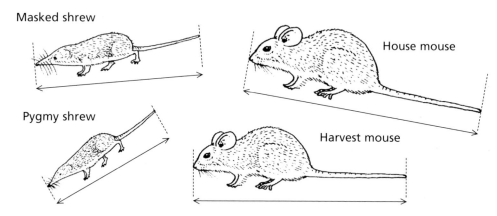

Masked shrew

House mouse

Pygmy shrew

Harvest mouse

2 (a) Measure the length of each caterpillar in cm.

(b) Write them in order of length, smallest first.

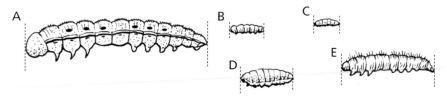

A

B

C

D

E

3 (a) Which of the lines below looks   (i) the longest

                                        (ii) the shortest

P ——————————

Q ———————————

R ———————————

S ——————————

T ——————————

(b) Measure the lines to see if you were right.
Write down the lengths of the longest and shortest lines.

Section B

1 What is the reading on each of these scales?

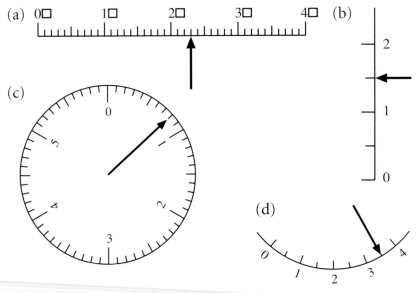

(a) 0□   1□   2□   3□   4□   (b)

(c)

(d)

2 Which number is each arrow pointing to?

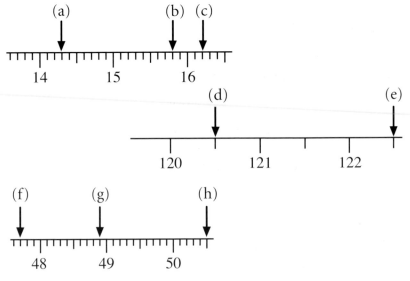

(a)   (b) (c)

14   15   16

(d)   (e)

120   121   122

(f)   (g)   (h)

48   49   50

Section C

1 The following list gives the weights of some blackcaps (birds) in grams.

    20, 18, 18.9, 17.6, 16.7, 19.6, 16.8, 23.1

Write down these weights in order, starting with the smallest.

2 Write each of these lists in order of size, smallest first.

(a) 4.6, 3.2, 2.9, 3, 0.7, 1   (b) 6.7, 5.9, 5, 10, 7, 8.1

(c) 0.3, 3.1, 5.9, 1.1, 3.5, 4   (d) 16.2, 3.9, 10, 4.8, 5, 17

3 The annual snowfall in inches in Buffalo, USA, is shown in the table below (every six years from 1912 to 1972).

Year	1912	1918	1924	1930	1936	1942	1948	1954	1960	1966	1972
Annual snowfall (inches)	78.1	110.5	46.7	79	103.9	89.6	39.9	89.9	115.6	98.3	110

Which of these years had

(a) the lowest snowfall

(b) the highest snowfall

(c) a snowfall less than 90 inches

(d) a snowfall greater than 100 inches

(e) a snowfall between 50 and 80 inches

4 This is part of a game where numbers have to be in order of size.

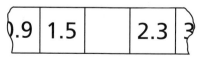

Which of these cards could be played in the space?

1.9   1.3   3.1   2   2.1

Mixed questions 3

Do not use a calculator for these questions.

1   There are 4 pairs of parallel lines here.
    There are 2 pairs of perpendicular lines.

    Check and write down which pairs are
    parallel and which are perpendicular.

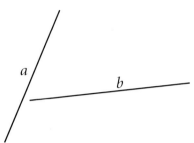

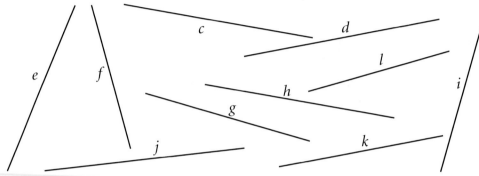

2   Draw this shape accurately.

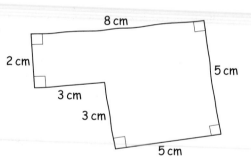

3   What number is each arrow pointing to?

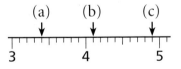
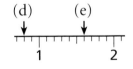
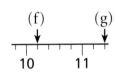

4   Write each list in order of size, smallest first.

    (a) 2.1, 1.9, 0.6, 7   (b) 5, 1.1, 0.1, 1.8   (c) 2.2, 0.6, 1.4, 2

5

A	B	E	G	I	L	R	T
2	3	4	5	6	7	8	9

Work out the answers to each of these.
Use the code and rearrange the letters in each part
to find the name of an animal.

(a) 36 ÷ 4   24 ÷ 6   20 ÷ 4   32 ÷ 4   42 ÷ 7

(b) 18 ÷ 3   16 ÷ 4   30 ÷ 6   49 ÷ 7   72 ÷ 9   27 ÷ 9

(c) 30 ÷ 5   48 ÷ 6   63 ÷ 7   21 ÷ 7   16 ÷ 8   30 ÷ 10

6 (a) Ravi packs eggs into boxes of 6. He has 123 eggs.
How many boxes can he fill?

(b) Chloe wants 29 crackers for Christmas. They come in boxes of 6.
How many boxes does she need to buy?

(c) My pet crocodile eats 9 sugar mice each day.
How many days will 50 sugar mice last her?

7 (a) Bob is going to school in the morning.
He gets to the bus stop at a quarter to 8.
How long is it until the next bus comes?

(b) Jane gets to the stop at 5 past 2
in the afternoon.
How long is it until the next bus?

(c) If I just miss the bus at 14:55,
how long is it until the next bus?

Buses leave at
06:55
08:05
10:35
14:55
16:20
18:45

8 (a) These shapes are called bracelets.
They are made from grey and white tiles.
Copy and complete this table.

No. of grey tiles	1	2	3	4	5
No. of white tiles					

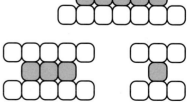

(b) How many white tiles do you need
for a bracelet with 10 greys?

(c) How many white tiles do
you need for 100 greys?

65

26 Number patterns

Sections B and C

1   What number is on the bottom of this dice?

2   There are three numbers you cannot see on this dice.
   What do the three numbers add up to?

3   What do the hidden numbers add up to on each of these dice?

(a)   (b)   (c)

4   Work out the total of all the numbers you cannot see in each of these
   pictures.

(b) 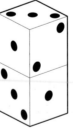   (c)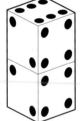

(a)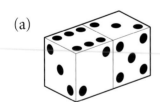

5   A square is magic when all its rows,
   its columns and its diagonals add up
   to the same number.

   Copy and complete this magic square.

		4	
8			10
		16	3
12	7	9	6

Sections D and E

1 Draw a different rectangle pattern with the same number of dots as each of these.

(a)
• • • • • • • •
• • • • • • • •

(b)
• • • • • • • •
• • • • • • • •
• • • • • • • •
• • • • • • • •

2 Find as many ways as you can to make rectangle patterns for these. (You need not draw the patterns. Just write, for example '4 × 2'.)

(a) 8   (b) 28   (c) 12   (d) 36

3 Is 9 a prime number? Explain.

4 In each of these lists, one number is prime. Write it down.

(a) 23, 24, 25, 26, 27   (b) 25, 26, 27, 28, 29   (c) 6, 7, 8, 9, 10

5 Work out which numbers are prime in each of these lists.

(a) 29, 30, 31, 32, 33   (b) 38, 39, 40, 41, 42   (c) 45, 46, 47, 48, 49

6 Work these out.

(a) 3^2 (b) 7^2 (c) 9^2 (d) 10^2

7 Work these out.

(a) 40^2 (b) 70^2 (c) 90^2

8 Afzal says that 5^2 is a prime number.
Explain why he cannot be right.

9 Work these out.

(a) $4^2 - 3^2$ (b) $5^2 - 3^2$ (c) $6^2 + 1^2$ (d) $10^2 - 8^2$

10 Which of the numbers on these cards are square numbers?

16   24   1   9   32   25   27   2

Section F

1. (a) What are the next two numbers?

    2, 6, 10, 14, 18, ..., ...

   (b) How did you work them out?

2. Work out the next two numbers.
   Write down the rule for working them out.

   (a) **10, 13, 16, 19, 22, ..., ...**

   (b) **50, 46, 42, 38, 34, ..., ...**

   (c) **15, 28, 41, 54, 67, ..., ...**

   (d) **100, 89, 78, 67, 56, ..., ...**

3. Work out the missing numbers.

   (a) **10, 16, 22, ..., 34, ..., 46**

   (b) **25, 28, ..., ..., 37, ..., 43**

   (c) **..., 20, 26, ..., 38, 44, ...**

   (d) **50, 47, ..., ..., 38, 35, ...**

4. Here is a set of cards.
   One card is missing. What number is on it?

   | **5** | **8** | **11** | **14** | **20** | **23** | **26** |

5. Two cards are missing from each of these sets.
   What numbers are on them?

   (a)

   | **50** | **46** | **42** | **34** | **30** | **22** | **18** |

   (b)

   | **10** | **22** | **28** | **34** | **40** | **52** | **58** |

27 Rectangles

Sections A and B

1   In this diagram ABCD is a rectangle.
    Write 'true' or 'false' for each of these
    statements.

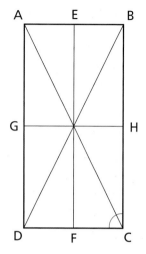

(a) The angle marked at point C
     in the rectangle is a right angle.

(b) Line AC is a line of symmetry of
     the rectangle.

(c) Side AD is perpendicular to side DC.

(d) Line GH is a line of symmetry of
     the rectangle.

(e) The rectangle has four lines of symmetry.

2   The rectangle KLMN is drawn
    on a coordinate grid.

    Write down the coordinates
    of these points.

    (a) K   (b) L   (c) M   (d) N

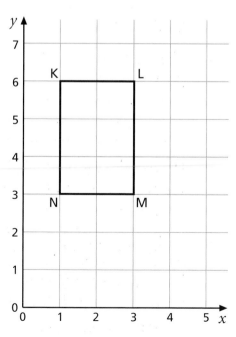

3   Copy the grid and rectangle
    on to squared paper.
    Draw all the lines of symmetry of
    the rectangle on your diagram.

4   The rectangle is translated 2 squares
    to the right and 3 squares down.
    Draw the new position of the
    rectangle on your diagram.

5   What are the new coordinates of
    point M after the translation?

㉙ Calculating with decimals

Sections A and B

Do not use a calculator in this section.

Work these out. Do them in your head if you can.

1 (a) 6.1 + 4.5　　(b) 2.7 + 4.7　　(c) 3.6 + 3　　(d) 6 + 6.3

2 (a) 7.8 − 6.4　　(b) 6.5 − 5.6　　(c) 4.8 − 3　　(d) 5 − 0.5

3 (a) 7.2 + 0.7　　(b) 0.6 + 6.4　　(c) 3.6 − 3　　(d) 6 − 1.3

For each of the questions 4 to 7, one part has a different answer
from the other two parts. Write the 'odd answer out'.

4 (a) 5.7 + 3.4　　(b) 4.6 + 4.3　　(c) 8.7 + 0.4

5 (a) 6.8 + 5.8　　(b) 9.7 + 2.5　　(c) 4.4 + 7.8

6 (a) 9.3 − 2.7　　(b) 8.5 − 1.9　　(c) 7.4 − 0.9

7 (a) 9 − 5.8　　(b) 7.2 − 3.9　　(c) 5.1 − 1.8

8 (a) What is the total length
of the two bars?

(b) Work out the length *b*.

7.6 cm

4.8 cm

b cm

9 Dilesh walks 8.2 km before lunch and 5.6 km after lunch.

(a) How far does he walk altogether?

(b) How much further does he walk in the morning?

10 Andy and Fi have a fishing competition.
Andy catches three fish. They weigh 1.2 kg, 2.3 kg and 0.8 kg.
Fi catches four fish that weigh 0.7 kg, 1.6 kg, 1.4 kg and 0.8 kg.

(a) What weight of fish did they each catch?

(b) Who had the bigger total, and by how much?

Section C

Do not use a calculator in this section.

1 How much will these bags of potatoes weigh altogether?

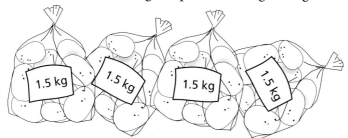

2 How much will these pieces of cheese weigh altogether?

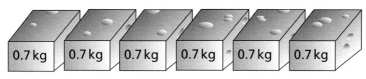

3 Work these out.
   (a) 0.8 × 3   (b) 0.6 × 5   (c) 0.5 × 8   (d) 0.5 × 7
   (e) 0.2 × 2   (f) 0.3 × 5   (g) 0.9 × 2   (h) 0.7 × 3

4 Work these out.
   (a) 3.4 × 2   (b) 2.1 × 6   (c) 5.6 × 2   (d) 5.2 × 7
   (e) 1.8 × 3   (f) 6.4 × 8   (g) 0.9 × 6   (h) 6.3 × 9

5 Tamera wants to make 6 tablecloths.
   She needs 3.4 metres of material for each tablecloth.

   How much material does she need altogether?

6 Jim wants to put ribbon round 9 cakes.
   He needs 0.7 metres of ribbon for each cake.

   How much ribbon does he need altogether?

7 A lift can carry up to 370 kilograms.
Adam has 8 boxes, each weighing 46.2 kg.

Can the lift carry all the boxes at once?
Show all your working.

Sections D and E

Do not use a calculator in this section.

1 Round these to the nearest whole number.
   (a) 4.9   (b) 15.4   (c) 19.6   (d) 5.5

2 Round these to the nearest ten.
   (a) 42   (b) 57   (c) 197   (d) 1997

3 Round these to the nearest hundred.
   (a) 2345   (b) 7654   (c) 64   (d) 350

4 (a) Round 2683 to the nearest ten.
   (b) Round 8889 to the nearest hundred.
   (c) Round 400.7 to the nearest whole number.
   (d) Round 6304 to the nearest ten.

5 (a) Estimate the answer to this calculation, by rounding.
        5.9 + 2.2 + 7.8 + 4.3
   (b) Now do the sum. Is the answer close to your estimate?

6 Estimate the answer to each of these, by rounding.
   Then do the calculation and compare the result with your estimate.
   (a) 3.7 + 2.4 + 8.1   (b) 7.7 + 4.1 + 0.5
   (c) 17.4 − 3.8   (d) 24 − 9.6
   (e) 8.3 + 4.5 + 6.5 + 5.2   (f) 3.2 + 8.4 + 5 + 1.3
   (g) 3.9 × 4   (h) 1.8 × 6
   (i) 5.9 × 3   (j) 7.8 × 4

Sections F and G

1 What do these figures stand for?

    (a) The **5** in **254.8**   (b) The **8** in **254.8**   (c) The **6** in **3627.9**

2 Do these in your head.

    (a) Add 1 to 32.7   (b) Add 0.1 to 32.7   (c) Add 10 to 32.7

    (d) Add 0.1 to 106.4   (e) Add 10 to 106.4   (f) Add 1 to 106.4

3 Do these in your head.

    (a) 47.6 + 1   (b) 47.6 + 10   (c) 47.6 + 0.1

    (d) 274.5 + 10   (e) 274.5 + 1   (f) 274.5 + 0.1

4 Write each of these as a decimal.

    (a) $3\frac{3}{10}$ (b) $4\frac{7}{10}$ (c) $6\frac{1}{10}$ (d) $8\frac{9}{10}$

5 Write these using fractions.

    (a) 1.7   (b) 0.9   (c) 6.3   (d) 2.1

6 Do these without using a calculator.

    (a) 6.8×10 (b) 0.6×10 (c) 10×1.8 (d) 10×31.5

    (e) 4.5×10 (f) 10×0.2 (g) 20.6×10 (h) 10×1.1

7 Do these without using a calculator.

    (a) $75 \div 10$ (b) $16 \div 10$ (c) $8 \div 10$ (d) $147 \div 10$

    (e) $4 \div 10$ (f) $20 \div 10$ (g) $3 \div 10$ (h) $99 \div 10$

8 Do these without using a calculator.

    (a) 49×10 (b) $49 \div 10$ (c) $603 \div 10$ (d) 10×10.6

    (e) $521 \div 10$ (f) $32 \div 10$ (g) 2.7×10 (h) 10×1.9

30 Chance

Section C

1 The four aces, the queen of hearts
   and the jack of spades from a pack
   of cards are shuffled.
   A player chooses a card without looking.

   Use the words in one of these boxes to describe the probability
   of each of these happening.

   | Impossible | Unlikely | 50% chance | Likely | Certain |

   (a) Choosing the queen   (b) Choosing an ace

   (c) Choosing a red card   (d) Choosing a king

2 Draw a probability scale from 0 to 1, about 10 cm long.
   Mark these roughly on your scale with arrows.

   (a) The probability it will get dark tonight

   (b) The probability of choosing an ace from a
       face-down pack of cards

   (c) The probability of getting an odd number when you
       roll a dice

3 Ten balls with the numbers 1 to 10 on them are placed in a bag.
   A ball is chosen without looking.
   Which of these arrows shows the probabilities below?

   (a) Choosing a ball with an even number

   (b) Choosing the ball with 10 on it

   (c) Choosing a number less than 9

Section D

1   With this spinner, what is
    the probability that

    (a) grey wins

    (b) black wins

    (c) white wins

    (d) white does not win

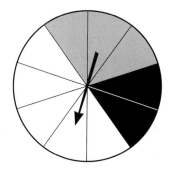

2   What is the probability of grey winning on each
    of these spinners?

(a)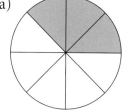

(b)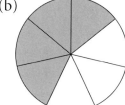

(c)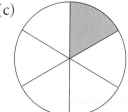

(d)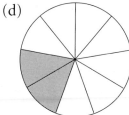

3   What is the probability of **not** getting grey in each
    of the spinners in question 2?

31 Negative numbers

Section A

1 Put these temperatures in order, lowest first.

A Inside a normal freezer

B Water from the hot tap

C Sea temperature in Cornwall in summer

D A garden pond in winter

E Oil when frying chips

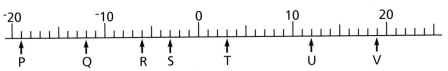

2 Match each of these temperatures to an arrow on the number line.
   (a) In Madrid, it is ⁻6°C.
   (b) In my greenhouse it is 12°C.
   (c) On the ski-slope in the morning, it was ⁻12°C.
   (d) When skiing in the afternoon it was ⁻3°C.
   (e) In Moscow in February, it was ⁻19°C.

3 In each of these, say which temperature is lowest.
   (a) ⁻12°C, ⁻6°C, ⁻10°C   (b) 1°C, ⁻4°C, ⁻2°C

4 In each of these, say which temperature is highest.
   (a) ⁻12°C, ⁻14°C, 0°C   (b) 1°C, ⁻4°C, ⁻20°C

5 Copy and complete these statements using > or < in the spaces.
   (a) 8°C ... 5°C   (b) 4°C ... 12°C   (c) ⁻2°C ... 5°C
   (d) ⁻7°C ... ⁻5°C   (e) 4°C ... ⁻6°C   (f) ⁻3°C ... ⁻5°C

6 This notice is displayed in a plant nursery.

   Which of these temperatures are
   suitable for the plants?

   | IMPORTANT |
   | These plants must be |
   | kept at > ⁻5°C |

   ⁻4°C   3°C   ⁻6°C   ⁻1°C   5°C   ⁻10°C

Sections B and C

1 The temperature in Barcelona is 2°C.

   (a) In Zurich, the temperature is 6 degrees higher. What temperature is it?

   (b) What temperature is it in London, 10 degrees lower than Barcelona?

2 What temperature is 6 degrees lower than 11°C?

3 What temperature is 11 degrees lower than 1°C?

4 What temperature is 8 degrees higher than ⁻2°C?

5 What temperature is 12 degrees higher than ⁻21°C?

6 What temperature is 15 degrees lower than ⁻21°C?

7 Make a true sentence by putting one of these numbers into each space.

    20   0   5   ⁻15   10

   A temperature of ....°C is .... degrees higher than a temperature of ....°C.

8 For London the lowest recorded temperature is ⁻10°C.
The highest recorded is 37°C.

   What is the difference between these temperatures?

9 The table shows the coldest temperature for each month in the UK, during the last century.

J	F	M	A	M	J	J	A	S	O	N	D
⁻27°C	⁻25°C	⁻22°C	⁻15°C	⁻9°C	⁻5°C	⁻2°C	⁻5°C	⁻7°C	⁻12°C	⁻23°C	⁻27°C

   (a) In which months was the temperature lowest?

   (b) Which month had the least cold temperature?

   (c) What was the difference between the coldest temperatures for February and August?

Section D

Julie has a thermometer which tells her the maximum and minimum temperatures in her garden each day.
This graph shows the temperatures she records for the first week in January.

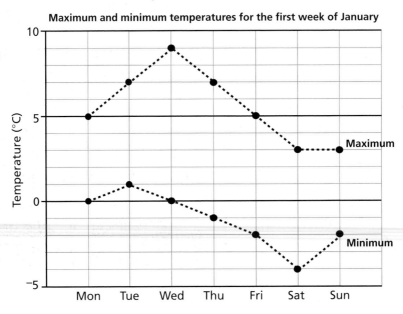

Maximum and minimum temperatures for the first week of January

1   What was the maximum temperature on Thursday?

2   What was the minimum temperature on Friday?

3   On which day was the maximum temperature highest?

4   On which day was the minimum temperature lowest?

5   What was the difference between the maximum
    and minimum temperatures on
    (a) Monday   (b) Friday   (c) Saturday

6   Which day had the biggest difference between the maximum
    and minimum temperatures?

32 Action and result puzzles

1 These are cards for the 15 puzzle.

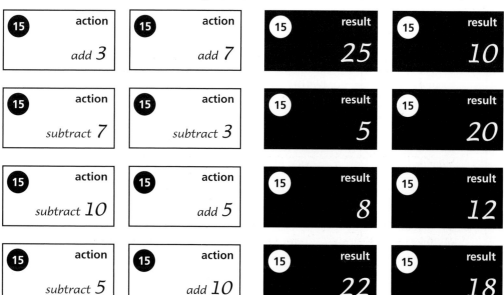

15	action	15	action
	add 3		*add 7*

Match the action and result cards.
Record your answers in a table like this.

15 puzzle	
Action	Result

2 What result would each of these actions have in the 15 puzzle?

(a) *subtract 9* (b) *add 9*

3 What action would give each of these results in the 15 puzzle?

(a) 17 (b) 21 (c) 4

4 Here are the cards for the 20 puzzle.

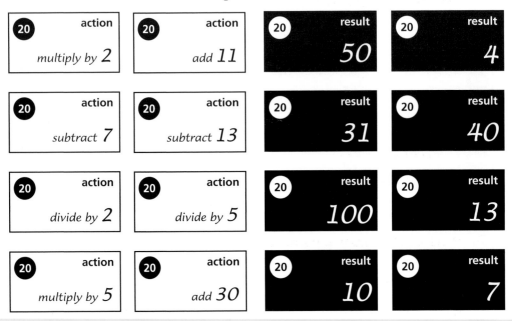

Match the action and result cards.
Record your answers in a table like this.

20 puzzle	
Action	Result

5 What result would each of these actions have in the 20 puzzle?

  (a) *subtract 9*   (b) *add 10*

  (c) *divide by 4*   (d) *multiply by 6*

6 What action would give each of these results in the 20 puzzle?

  (a) 15   (b) 33   (c) 80

7 In the 20 puzzle more than one action would give 60.
  Give two of these.

Mixed questions 4

Do not use a calculator for these questions.

1 This is a rectangle pattern made from 30 dots.

   (a) Draw a different rectangle pattern
       with 30 dots.

   (b) Write down another pair of
       factors of 30.

   (c) Is 30 a square number? Explain.

2 Work these out.   (a) 9^2 (b) $8^2 - 6^2$ (c) 60^2

3 Work out the missing numbers in each of these.
   Write down the rule for working them out.

   (a) 5, 9, 13, 17, 21, ..., ...   (b) 85, 79, 73, 67, ..., ...

   (c) 34, 39, ..., 49, 54, ...   (d) 45, ..., 37, ..., 29, ...

4 A mail order firm supplies organic fertiliser in three sizes.

Small	Medium	Large
1.8 kg	3.6 kg	7 kg

   (a) How much do one small and one medium bag weigh together?

   (b) How much more does the medium bag weigh than the small bag?

   (c) How much more does the large bag weigh than the medium bag?

   (d) How much do four medium bags weigh altogether?

5 Estimate the answer to each of these, by rounding.
   Then do the calculation and compare the answer with your estimate.

   (a) 3.7 + 2.2 + 5.8   (b) 18.7 − 7.9   (c) 3.7 × 5

6 Work these out.

   (a) 45.5 + 1   (b) 27.6 + 0.1   (c) 127.3 + 10   (d) 254.3 + 0.1

7 Work these out.

   (a) 3.8 × 10   (b) 10 × 24.6   (c) 265 ÷ 10   (d) 39 ÷ 10

8 Which letter on this probability scale shows the probability of each of the events below?

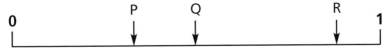

(a) Choosing a red card from a pack of cards.

(b) Rolling a number less than 3 with a dice.

(c) Picking a red sweet from a bag of eight sweets which has seven red and one yellow sweet.

9 This spinner has diamonds, hearts and clubs on its sections.

With this spinner, what is the probability that

(a) a club wins   (b) a heart wins

(c) a diamond wins   (d) a diamond does not win

10 On a cold day in February, Dermot measured the temperature around his home.

This table shows the temperature in some of the places.

Place	Temperature
Kitchen	9°C
Garden	⁻8°C
Conservatory	5°C
Living room	15°C
Patio	⁻2°C

(a) Which place was warmest?

(b) Which place was coldest?

(c) How many degrees warmer was the conservatory than the patio?

(d) Which was warmer, the patio or the garden?
By how many degrees?

(e) The garage was 5 degrees warmer than the patio.
What was the temperature in the garage?

11 Write these temperatures in order, coldest first.

⁻4°C   8°C   ⁻7°C   10°C   0°C   ⁻2°C

12 Copy and complete each of these, using either > or < .

(a) 5°C ... 8°C   (b) 7°C ... ⁻5°C   (c) ⁻4°C ... ⁻7°C

33 Two decimal places

Sections B and C

1   These scales are marked in litres.
    What amount is shown in each one?

(a) 0.4
     0.3

(b) 1.3
     1.2

(c) 1
     0.9

(d) 0.1
     0

(e) 3.6
     3.5

2   What number does each arrow point to?

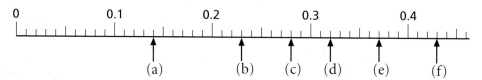

3   What number does each arrow point to?

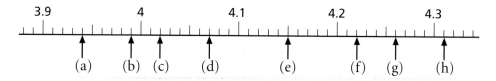

4   What number is halfway between
    (a) 4.1 and 4.2   (b) 4.2 and 4.3   (c) 4 and 4.1   (d) 3.9 and 4

5   Copy the number line below on squared paper.
    Draw arrows to show where these numbers are.

        2.86   3.13   3.01   3.08   2.93

        2.8   2.9   3   3.1

Section D

Tenths

| 0 | 0.1 | 0.2 | 0.3 | 0.4 | 0.5 | 0.6 | 0.7 | 0.8 | 0.9 | 1 |

| 0 | 0.10 | 0.20 | 0.30 | 0.40 | 0.50 | 0.60 | 0.70 | 0.80 | 0.90 | 1 |

Hundredths

1 (a) What number is halfway between 0.50 and 0.60?

(b) What number is halfway between 0.2 and 0.3?

(c) What number is halfway between 0 and 0.10?

(d) What number is halfway between 0.4 and 0.5?

2 Sort these into four matching pairs.

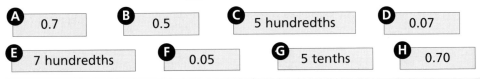

A 0.7   **B** 0.5   **C** 5 hundredths   **D** 0.07

E 7 hundredths   **F** 0.05   **G** 5 tenths   **H** 0.70

3 Write each list of numbers in order of size, smallest first.
Use the number lines above to help you.

(a) 0.11, 0.20, 0.04, 0.18, 0.5

(b) 0.34, 0.30, 0.59, 0.4, 0.80

(c) 0.9, 0.54, 0.40, 0.21, 0.07

(d) 0.1, 0.05, 0.17, 0.6, 0.3

4 Write each list of numbers in order of size, smallest first.
Try not to use the number lines to help you.

(a) 0.31, 0.26, 0.5, 0.40, 0.53

(b) 0.26, 0.20, 0.6, 0.59, 0.80

(c) 0.2, 0.9, 0.39, 0.09, 0.99

(d) 0.25, 0.87, 0.81, 0.9, 0.3

5 Write each list of numbers in order of size, smallest first.

(a) 2.39, 2.8, 2.07, 2.5   (b) 1.1, 1.01, 1.5, 1.43

Section E

1 Write these in metres.

   (a) 3 metres and 27 centimetres   (b) 1 metre and 56 cm

   (c) 5 metres and 64 cm   (d) 498 cm   (e) 209 cm

2 Find four matching pairs of lengths.

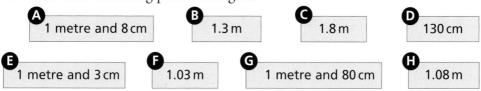

3 Write these in metres.

   (a) 2 metres and 9 cm   (b) 320 cm   (c) 4 metres and 80 cm

   (d) 9 metres and 1 cm   (e) 640 cm   (f) 604 cm

4 Copy and complete this table.
   It shows the heights of five people.

Name	Height in cm	Height in metres and cm	Height in metres
Mel	152 cm		
Ginger		1 m 49 cm	
Ali			1.59 m
Kay		1 m 9 cm	
Morag			1.6 m

5 Put these lists of lengths in order, shortest first.

   (a) 2.87 m, 3.1 m, 3.08 m, 2.9 m   (b) 0.9 m, 1.01 m, 0.05 m, 0.5 m

6 Fiona's height is between 1.5 and 1.6 metres.
   Which of these is a possible height for Fiona?

   A 1.48 m   **B** 1.57 m   **C** 153 cm   **D** 105 cm

Section F

1 Which of the numbers in the box are between 6.1 and 6.4?

7.15	6.3	0.62
6.17	6.37	6.05

2 Write each list of numbers in order of size, smallest first.

(a) 4.3, 5, 4.25, 4.09, 4.24

(b) 1.5, 0.7, 0.65, 0.08, 1

3 Find a word by arranging the numbers in order, smallest first.

L	E	N	T	A	G	R	I
0.6	0.79	0.4	0.01	0.23	0.51	0.04	0.2

4 These cards make the word 'DECIMAL' with the numbers in order.

D	E	C	I	M	A	L
5.4	6		6.5	6.56	6.7	7

Which of these numbers could be on the card marked 'C'?

6.6   5.9   6.06   6.48   6.51

5 This table gives the results of a high jump contest.

Name	Height of jump
Joe Hall	1.5 m
Suneet Patel	1.48 m
Pete Smith	1.06 m
Garry Fulton	1.59 m
Jamie White	1.6 m

(a) Who won the contest?

(b) Who came last?

(c) List all the people who jumped higher than 1.4 m.

Section G

1 The figure 4 in the number 5741.39 stands for 4 tens or 40.
What do these figures stand for?

(a) The 7   (b) The 3   (c) The 1   (d) The 9

2 Match each card on the left with a number on the right.
The same answer may be used twice.

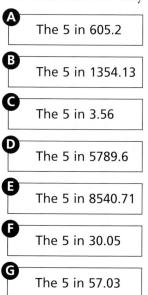
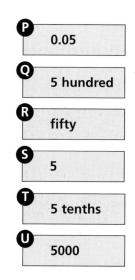

A The 5 in 605.2

B The 5 in 1354.13

C The 5 in 3.56

D The 5 in 5789.6

E The 5 in 8540.71

F The 5 in 30.05

G The 5 in 57.03

P 0.05

Q 5 hundred

R fifty

S 5

T 5 tenths

U 5000

3 Do these in your head.

(a) 62.7 + 1   (b) 62.7 + 10   (c) 62.7 + 0.2

(d) 39.74 − 1   (e) 39.74 − 6   (f) 39.74 − 0.1

(g) 39.74 − 0.01   (h) 29.1 + 1

4 Copy and complete these.

(a) 458.1 + **?** = 468.1   (b) 34.91 + **?** = 34.92   (c) 103.6 + **?** = 153.6

(d) 75.32 − **?** = 74.32   (e) 54.8 − **?** = 54   (f) 587.5 + **?** = 987.5

(g) 6.77 − **?** = 6.07   (h) 6.77 − **?** = 6.7

36 Is it an add?

Section B

Soft drinks

Economy pack
6 cans
£2.00

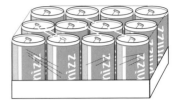

Family pack
12 cans
£3.00

Write the **calculation** for each question, not the answer.

1   You drink five of the cans from a family pack.
    How many cans are left in the pack?

2   You buy an economy pack and a family pack.
    How many cans do you buy?

3   How much would you have to pay for three family packs?

4   You buy a family pack and an economy pack.
    How much do you pay altogether?

5   How many cans are there in four family packs?

6   How much change will you get from £5 if you buy a family pack?

7   You need thirty cans of drink.
    How many economy packs would you have to buy?

8   Jim and Suzy split a family pack equally.
    How many do they get each?

Films

A - pack

£8.00
2 films
36 photographs
on each film

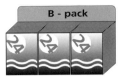

B - pack

£8.00
3 films
24 photographs
on each film

C - pack

£18.00
6 films
36 photographs
on each film

Write down the **calculation** for each question, not the answer.

1 You buy an A-pack and a B-pack.
   How many films do you buy?

2 How many more films do you get in a C-pack than in an A-pack?

3 You buy a C-pack and use two films.
   How many films are left?

4 You buy three A-packs. How much does it cost?

5 How many photographs can you take with an A-pack of films?

6 How many more photographs can you take with a film from
   an A-pack than a film from a B-pack?

7 You buy three B-packs. How many films do you buy?

8 How many films from a C-pack will you need to
   take 180 photographs?

9 How much does a film from an A-pack cost?

10 You are going on holiday and you want to take 18 films.
    How many C-packs will you have to buy?

Section C

1 Write down the calculation for each of these tales.

   (a) *Mr Faraday buys 12 multipacks of mineral water.*
   Each pack contains 6 bottles.
   How many bottles does he have altogether?

   (b) *Mary is putting eggs into boxes.*
   Each box holds six eggs.
   She has 120 eggs altogether.
   How many boxes will she need?

   (c) *Baljit has 15 Diwali cards to send.*
   His mother gives him another 6.
   How many does he now have?

   (d) *Maddi has 24 pairs of tights.*
   She throws away 5 pairs with holes in them.
   How many pairs does she have left?

2 What calculation would you have to do to find out the following?

   (a) How many days there are in 40 weeks

   (b) How many hours are left in a day if you
   sleep for eight of them

   (c) How many minutes there are in 420 seconds

   (d) The number of pupils in a class of 15 boys and 17 girls

   (e) How many times you have to run around a 400 m track
   to have run 2000 m

   (f) The total distance you swim if you swim 64 lengths
   of a 25 m swimming pool

3 Make up a tale or a problem for which the calculation would be

   (a) 50×12 (b) $80 \div 10$ (c) $24 + 15$ (d) $36 - 8$

Section D

1   Do these on a calculator and check each answer.
    Write down the calculation you did to check your answer.

    (a) 352 + 579   (b) 187 + 345 + 278   (c) 437 − 243

    (d) 3124 − 1794   (e) 26 × 47   (f) 347 × 36

    (g) 513 ÷ 19   (h) 1734 ÷ 34

In each of the following questions
   • write down the calculation you are going to do
   • work out the answer with a calculator
   • check your answer and write down the calculation you did to check

2   Pupils in Year 7 at Growham High School are collecting computer
    vouchers from a local supermarket.
    The number of vouchers collected by each class is

    7S 578   **7T** 1253   **7M** 1820   **7N** 2176   **7P** 987

    (a) How many vouchers were collected altogether?

    (b) How many more vouchers than 7T did 7N collect?

    (c) There are 28 pupils in class 7M.
        If the vouchers were shared equally between the 28 pupils,
        how many would each pupil get?

3   A corner shop buys tubes of tropical fruit sweets.
    Each tube contains 15 sweets.
    The tubes are packed in boxes. Each box contains 144 tubes.

    (a) How many sweets are there in the box altogether?

    (b) The shop sells 87 tubes from one box.
        How many tubes are left in the box?

    Tropical fruits can also be bought in bags with 40 sweets in.
    The shop buys these in boxes of 55 bags.

    (c) How many sweets are there in a box of 55 bags?

    (d) Which contains more sweets, a box of tubes or a box of bags?

③⑦ Graphs and charts

Section A

1   Halley High School carried out a survey.
    Year 7 and year 11 pupils were asked how they got to school.
    This chart shows the results as percentages.

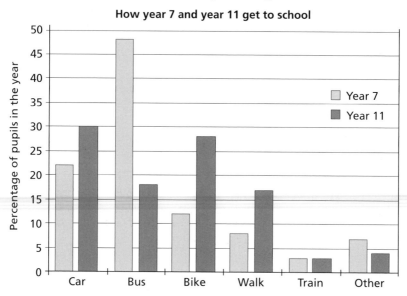

(a) What was the most common way for year 7 pupils to
    get to school?

(b) What was the most common way for year 11?

(c) What percentage of year 11 pupils came by car?

(d) Roughly what percentage of year 7 pupils walked?

(e) Did more year 7 pupils come by car or by bike?

(f) For year 11 which was more common, to come by bike or by bus?

(g) In year 8, 20% of the pupils came by bike.
    Is this more or less than year 7?

(h) In year 8, $\frac{1}{4}$ of the pupils came by car.
    Is this more or less than year 7?

Section C

1 The graph below shows the temperatures in °C in three cities.
   It shows the temperatures at noon in Sydney, London and Madrid.
   The graph covers 15 days in May.

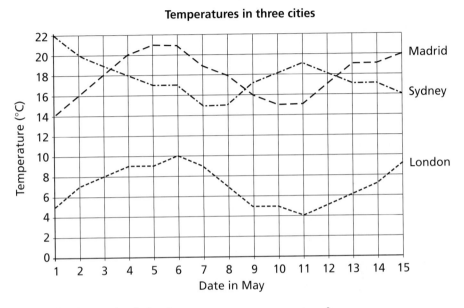

Temperatures in three cities

(a) Which city had the lowest noon temperature?
   What was it?

(b) Which city had the highest temperature?
   What was it?

(c) The temperature in London went up, then fell to its lowest on the
   11th May, and then went up again.
   Describe what happened to the temperature in Sydney.

(d) Describe what happened to the temperature in Madrid.

(e) What is the highest temperature in London shown on the graph?

(f) What is the lowest temperature in Madrid shown?

(g) On which dates was it hotter at noon in Madrid than in Sydney?

Section D

1 The chart shows what sort of jobs people had
   in nine countries in the European Union in 1996.

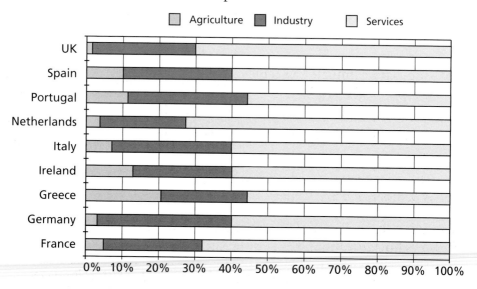

Source: Regional Trends 1996

(a) Which country had the smallest percentage of people employed
    in agriculture?

(b) Which country had most employed in agriculture?

(c) Which countries had the smallest percentage of
    people employed in services?

(d) Which country had most in services?

(e) Which country had most in industry?

(f) Which countries had 30% or more employed in industry?

(g) Which countries had 60% or less employed in services?

Section E

1 These figures show the weight of 30 fish caught in a pond.
The weights are all in grams.

17	56	34	18	19	54	8	45	43	21
33	38	32	21	41	36	32	28	29	30
42	51	18	55	12	10	40	39	27	44

(a) Copy and complete this table for the weights of the fish.

(b) Draw a bar chart showing the weight of the 30 fish.

Weight (g)	Tally	Frequency
0–9		
10–19		
20–29		

(c) Copy and complete this.

The most common weight of fish caught in this pond is between ... and ... grams.

2 This table shows the rainfall each month in Miami one year.
It shows how much rain fell each month in millimetres.

Jan	Feb	Mar	Apr	May	Jun	Jul	Aug	Sep	Oct	Nov	Dec
58	52	56	65	185	195	137	175	215	220	95	45

(a) Draw axes on graph paper like the ones on the right.

Plot the rainfall data as points on your graph.

Join the points with a dotted line.

(b) Write a sentence or two to describe the rainfall in Miami throughout the year.

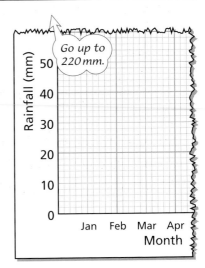

95

39 Working with fractions

Section A

1 There is 1 bar of chocolate at this table.
There are 4 people.
They share the chocolate equally.

What fraction of a bar do they each get?

2 At this table there are 2 bars of chocolate
and 6 people.

What fraction of a bar does each person get?

3 You join the people at this table.
Then the chocolate is shared out equally.

What fraction of a chocolate bar do you get?

4 In this picture, two people are sitting at table P
and four people are sitting at table Q.

(a) Who gets the most chocolate, a person
sitting at table P or a person at table Q?

(b) What fraction of a bar do they each get?

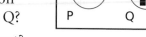

5 In each of the pictures below, who gets the most chocolate,
a person sitting at table P or a person at table Q?

Explain your reasons carefully.

(a) 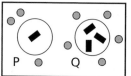 (b) 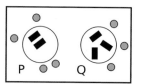 (c)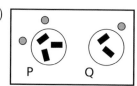

96

Section B

1   This chocolate bar shows the statement

   $\frac{1}{4}$ of 12 = 3

   Match each statement below with the correct bar.

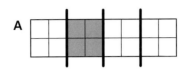

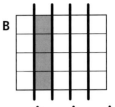

P $\frac{1}{5}$ of 20 = 4

Q $\frac{1}{4}$ of 16 = 4

R $\frac{1}{4}$ of 24 = 6

S $\frac{1}{7}$ of 21 = 3

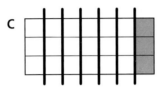

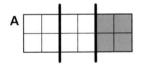

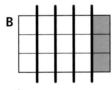

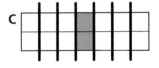

2   Write a statement for each of these bars.

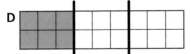

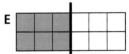

3   Draw a chocolate bar to show each of these.
   Work out each answer.

   (a) $\frac{1}{4}$ of 20   (b) $\frac{1}{6}$ of 30   (c) $\frac{1}{2}$ of 16   (d) $\frac{1}{7}$ of 28

4   Work these out.

   (a) $\frac{1}{4}$ of 28   (b) $\frac{1}{3}$ of 15   (c) $\frac{1}{8}$ of 32   (d) $\frac{1}{5}$ of 40

   (e) $\frac{1}{8}$ of 56   (f) $\frac{1}{7}$ of 63   (g) $\frac{1}{5}$ of 35   (h) $\frac{1}{9}$ of 54

   (i) $\frac{1}{6}$ of 12   (j) $\frac{1}{3}$ of 21   (k) $\frac{1}{7}$ of 28   (l) $\frac{1}{6}$ of 24

Section C

1 Match each statement with one of the diagrams.
   For example, **P** $\frac{2}{3}$ of 15 = 10 matches with **A**.

P $\frac{2}{3}$ of 15 = 10

Q $\frac{5}{6}$ of 12 = 10

R $\frac{3}{4}$ of 12 = 9

S $\frac{5}{6}$ of 18 = 15

T $\frac{3}{5}$ of 10 = 6

U $\frac{3}{4}$ of 16 = 12

2 Work these out.

   (a) $\frac{3}{4}$ of 36   (b) $\frac{3}{4}$ of 48   (c) $\frac{2}{3}$ of 27   (d) $\frac{2}{3}$ of 24

   (e) $\frac{3}{8}$ of 24   (f) $\frac{5}{6}$ of 30   (g) $\frac{3}{5}$ of 35   (h) $\frac{4}{9}$ of 36

   (i) $\frac{3}{4}$ of 4   (j) $\frac{3}{5}$ of 50   (k) $\frac{3}{10}$ of 600   (l) $\frac{3}{5}$ of 500

3 There are 36 members in a canoe club.

   (a) $\frac{1}{9}$ are instructors. How many is this?

   (b) $\frac{4}{9}$ of the members are female. How many is this?

   (c) $\frac{2}{3}$ of the members are under 21. How many is this?

   (d) $\frac{5}{6}$ of the members go canoeing every week. How many is that?

4 A church tower is 40 metres high.

   (a) $\frac{1}{4}$ of the way up the tower there is a window.
       How high off the ground is the window?

   (b) $\frac{3}{4}$ of the way up there is a clock.
       How high off the ground is the clock?

   (c) $\frac{3}{5}$ of the way up is a sundial.
       How high is this?

   (d) The church roof is $\frac{5}{8}$ the height of the tower. How high is the roof?

Section D

1 (a) Each of these shapes is $\frac{1}{3}$ of a circle.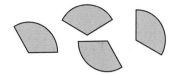
How many $\frac{1}{3}$s are there here?

(b) Write $\frac{4}{3}$ as a mixed number.

2 Use this diagram to
copy and complete
$2\frac{1}{3} = \frac{\blacksquare}{3}$

3 Copy and complete each of these.

(a) $1\frac{2}{3} = \frac{\blacksquare}{3}$ (b) $3\frac{1}{3} = \frac{\blacksquare}{3}$ (c) $\frac{13}{3} =$ (d) $\frac{8}{3} =$

4 For each of these diagrams, write a mixed number and
an improper fraction.

(a) 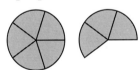   (b)

(c) 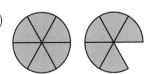   (d)

5 Copy and complete each of these.

(a) $1\frac{4}{5} = \frac{\blacksquare}{5}$ (b) $\frac{13}{5} = 2\frac{\blacksquare}{5}$ (c) $3\frac{1}{5} = \frac{\blacksquare}{5}$ (d) $3\frac{3}{5} = \frac{\blacksquare}{5}$

6 Write each of these as a mixed number.

(a) $\frac{11}{4}$ (b) $\frac{11}{3}$ (c) $\frac{11}{5}$ (d) $\frac{11}{7}$

7 Write each of these as an improper fraction.

(a) $2\frac{1}{7}$ (b) $3\frac{3}{8}$ (c) $5\frac{5}{6}$ (d) $6\frac{5}{7}$

40 3-D shapes

Section B

1 Which of these pentominoes can be folded to make an open cube?

(a)

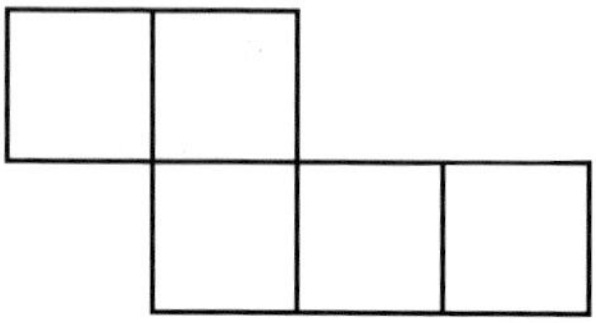

(b)

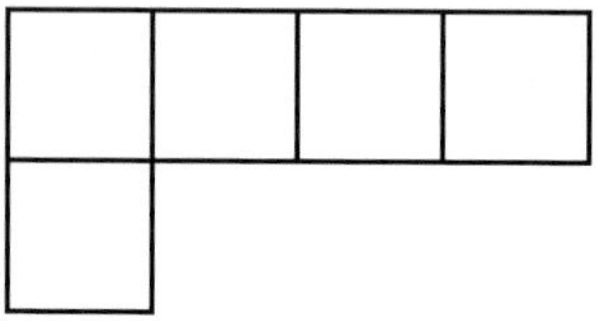

(c)

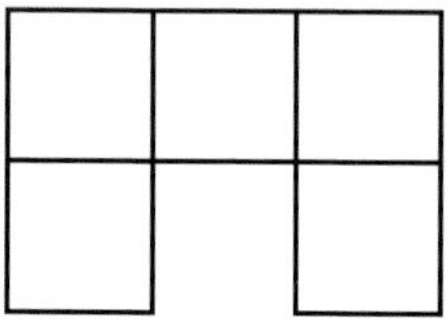

2 This is a net for an open cube.
It is folded so that the letters are on the outside.

Which of these are possible views of the open cube it makes?

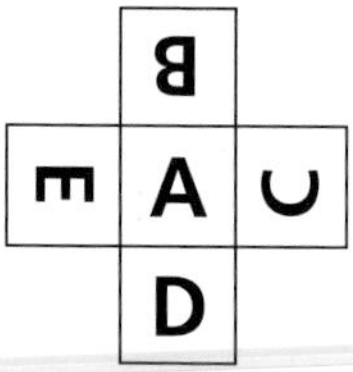

(a)

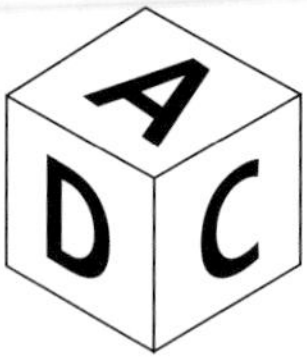

(b)

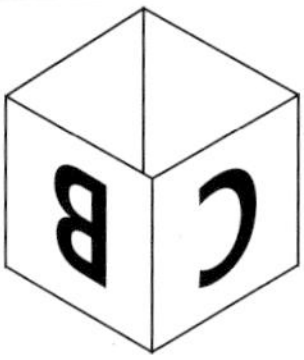

(c)

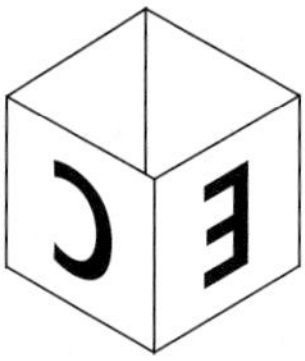

(d)

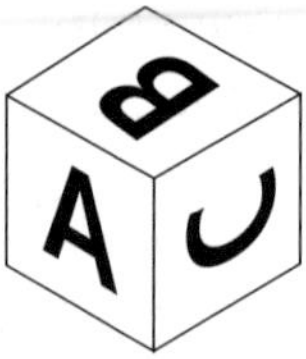

(e)

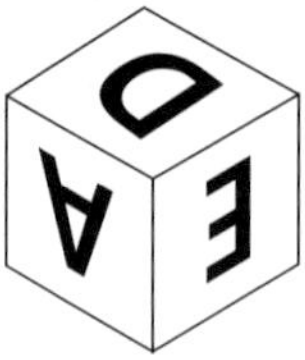

(f)

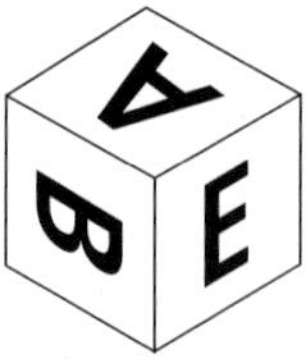

Section C

1   These shapes are all made from 4 cubes.
    Match them into four pairs which are the same shape.

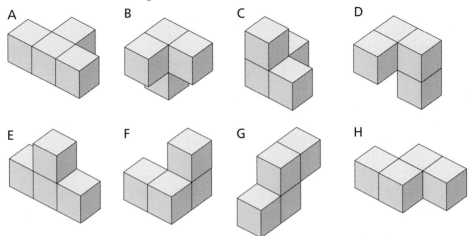

A   B   C   D

E   F   G   H

2   How many cubes would you need to make cuboids
    with these measurements?

    (a) 5 cubes long by 3 cubes wide and 2 cubes high

    (b) 8 cubes long by 5 cubes wide and 4 cubes high

3   Mrs England asks her class to make a cuboid which is
    4 cubes long by 3 cubes wide by 2 cubes high.

    These are some unfinished cuboids. There are no hidden gaps.
    How many cubes does each pupil need to finish their cuboid?

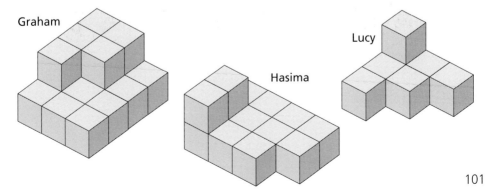

Graham

Hasima

Lucy

41 Ratio

Sections A and B

1 Here is a recipe for pasta sauce.

   (a) Luigi wants to make pasta sauce for two.

     (i) How many tins of tomatoes does he need?

     (ii) How many onions does he need?

   (b) Felizia wants to cook pasta sauce for 12. Write out a list of the things she will need.

Pasta sauce serves 4
2 tins tomatoes
6 medium onions
4 teaspoons tomato paste
2 teaspoons mixed herbs

Jam tarts makes 20
200 grams jam
200 grams plain flour
100 grams margarine
water as needed

2 The recipe on this card makes 20 jam tarts.

   (a) (i) How many grams of flour do you need to make one jam tart?

     (ii) How much flour do you need to make 8 tarts?

   (b) Write out a list of what you need to make 12 jam tarts.

3 This tells you what you need to make cranberry punch.

   (a) Mischa uses 2 litres of cranberry juice. How much of the other ingredients does she use?

   (b) How much cranberry punch does she make altogether?

Cranberry punch
1 part cranberry juice
2 parts orange juice
2 parts cola

4 Xavier and Yves are sharing some postcards. For every 1 card that Xavier gets, Yves gets 3 cards.

   (a) How many cards will Yves get if Xavier gets 5?

   (b) How many cards will Yves get if Xavier gets 40?

   (c) How many cards will Xavier get if Yves gets 60?

Mixed questions 5

1   What number does each arrow point to?

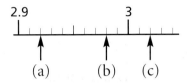

2   Write each list of numbers in order of size, smallest first.

(a) 0.68, 0.5, 0.48, 0.06, 0.60   (b) 3.54, 3.4, 3.05, 3.56, 3.50

3   Write the **calculation** for each
    question, not the answer.

(a) You drink 4 cartons from
    a large pack.
    How many cartons are left
    in the pack?

(b) How much would you have
    to pay for five triple packs?

(c) You need 24 cartons of juice.
    How many large packs would you have to buy?

4   Work these out.

(a) $\frac{3}{4}$ of 32   (b) $\frac{3}{5}$ of 20   (c) $\frac{5}{8}$ of 48   (d) $\frac{4}{10}$ of 250

5   Sonia has 48 DVDs.

(a) $\frac{1}{6}$ of these are comedy films. How many is this?

(b) $\frac{3}{8}$ of the DVDs are nature programmes. How many is this?

(c) $\frac{2}{3}$ of the DVDs were bought this year. How many is that?

6   Copy and complete each of these.

(a) $2\frac{1}{3} = \frac{}{3}$ (b) $3\frac{2}{5} = \frac{}{5}$ (c) $\frac{13}{3} =$ (d) $\frac{17}{6} =$

7   This table shows the hottest temperature each month
    in Cairo one year in °C.

Jan	Feb	Mar	Apr	May	Jun	Jul	Aug	Sep	Oct	Nov	Dec
17	19	21	27	32	35	37	35	32	30	25	20

(a) Draw axes on graph paper
    like the ones on the right.

    Plot the temperature as points
    on your graph.

    Join the points with a line.

(b) In which months was the hottest
    temperature less than 20°C?

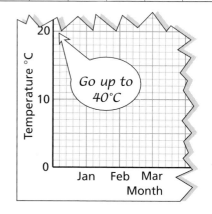

8   An open cube is made from this net.

    Which of these is not a view of the cube?

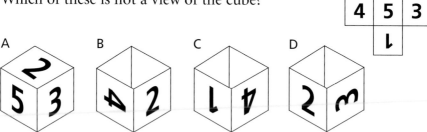

9   This tells you how to make mortar.

(a) Patrick puts 4 buckets of cement in
    his cement mixer.

    How much of the other ingredients
    does he need to use?

(b) How many buckets does he put in the mixer altogether?

Mortar mix
2 buckets of cement
8 buckets of sand
1 bucket of water